COMET'S TALE

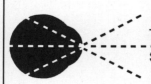

This Large Print Book carries the
Seal of Approval of N.A.V.H.

Comet's Tale

HOW THE DOG I RESCUED SAVED MY LIFE

Steven D. Wolf
with Lynette Padwa

THORNDIKE PRESS

A part of Gale, Cengage Learning

GALE
CENGAGE Learning·

Detroit • New York • San Francisco • New Haven, Conn • Waterville, Maine • London

GALE
CENGAGE Learning

LIBRARY OF CONGRESS CATALOGING-IN-PUBLICATION DATA

Wolf, Steven D., 1954–
    Comet's tale : how the dog I rescued saved my life / Steven D. Wolf,
Lynette Padwa.
        p. cm. — (Thorndike press large print nonfiction)
    ISBN-13: 978-1-4104-5567-3 (hardback)
    ISBN-10: 1-4104-5567-X (hardcover)
    1. Dog rescue—Anecdotes. 2. Racing greyhound—Anecdotes.
3. Greyhounds—Anecdotes. 4. Dog adoption—Anecdotes. 5. Dogs—
Therapeutic use. 6. Dog owners—Biography. 7. Service dogs—Anecdotes.
8. Human-animal relationships. 9. Wolf, Steven D., 1954– 10. Large type
books. I. Padwa, Lynette. II. Title.
HV4746.W65 2013
636.7'0832092—dc23   2012043989

Published in 2013 by arrangement with Algonquin Books of Chapel
Hill, a division of Workman Publishing Co., Inc.

Printed in the United States of America
1 2 3 4 5 6 7 17 16 15 14 13

FOR FREDERIQUE,
a wonderfully rare woman
who brought exceptional meaning
to what is often considered a
passé promise —
In sickness and in health.

PROLOGUE

March 2000 — Arizona

It was just past 8:00 a.m. and the road winding through the foothills north of Flagstaff was deserted. The spring air was chilly, but I rolled down the window anyway, letting the fragrant scent of Ponderosa pine rush through the car. Every so often a vista would open up and the snowy peaks of Mount Elden would appear, etched and highlighted in the sharp morning sun like a woodblock print. Then the road would curve away, the view would close, and I'd lean forward, searching for the turnoff to the foster family's ranch.

Finally I saw it — a weather-beaten two-story house with a high-pitched roof and covered porch. It sat on a parcel of flat, grassy land the size of a football field, entirely surrounded by a high post-and-wire fence. I parked outside the gate and slowly got out, gripping my canes and bracing for the pain in my spine. Breathing hard, I leaned against the car. The air was still. At the far end of the field I glimpsed a spot of movement. In the same instant I noticed a faint rhythmic beat, like distant drumming. The spot moved closer, my eyes adjusted, and a pack of greyhounds materialized, jetting around the inside perimeter of the fence. The drumbeat deepened to thunder. A few seconds later they streaked past me, thigh muscles bunched, hind paws stretching toward shoulders, mud flying in their wake, individual dogs blurring into a mass of muscle that flowed like mercury.

Thrilled, I watched them rocket away, racing for the sheer exhilaration of it. *Just like children,* I thought. *Kids set loose on the first spring day after a long winter.* I could almost detect laughter.

"We never grow tired of watching," a woman's voice called from across the muddy field. I had been so focused on the greyhounds that I hadn't noticed the young foster mom ambling toward me, her hands shoved in the pockets of faded blue jeans. "So glad you decided to drive up after all," she said when she reached me. "I'm Kathy. Come on, I'll introduce you to the pack."

As soon as we turned back to the house, the dogs veered in our direction. Within seconds I was surrounded by panting, jostling greyhounds. The group seemed to contain every shade in the animal kingdom — soft fawns, striking brindles, deep reds, bold black-and-whites, and the famous steel gray, often referred to as blue. Their only common marking was the white patch on each dog's chest. The hounds nudged and bumped each other as they vied for my attention, but the competition was friendly, no growling or biting. It reminded me of my yearly reunion with my own pack of cousins.

After weeks of hemming and hawing about it, I had come here prepared to adopt, but I hadn't realized what a pack of greyhounds really meant — the number and variety, each dog an individual with its own full-grown personality. It wasn't like choosing a puppy. Kathy and I stood in the yard watching them for a half hour, but no single animal stood out as "mine." At last, with some hesitation, I pointed out a fawn-colored hound who flitted on the fringe of the group. "What about that one?" I asked. The dog's caramel eyes were lively, and she struck me as a feisty yet refined lady who might be easy to live with and also play well with others. It was just me here in Arizona, in exile from my family back in Nebraska, where the winters were too cold for my degenerative back condition. Still, any dog would have to interact with our rowdy pair of golden retrievers when I returned home for the summers.

"Let's see how she does indoors," said Kathy.

It was warm and snug inside the house. A sofa and a few comfortable chairs were pushed back against the living room walls, leaving plenty of space for the greyhounds to romp. In a far corner stood a black wood-burning stove, heat shimmering around it. I made my way to the sofa and awkwardly settled in, letting my canes drop to the floor in front of me.

The fawn-colored racer pranced over to me, ready to play. She executed a short jump, landed directly in front of me, and lowered her head, inviting me to pet her. I stroked her gently, surprised at the wiriness of her sleek fur. She wagged her tail and I scratched between her ears.

"What would I need to do if I were going to take a dog home today?" I asked. While Kathy talked about adoption fees and vet care, I wondered what treats I could buy for my new pet. Did greyhounds like liver or did they prefer lamb?

"Then you just write a check and the

hound is yours," Kathy finished.

I hesitated again. A little voice inside my head — my wife Freddie's voice, to be exact — protested, *Are you out of your mind? You cannot seriously be considering adopting a greyhound. You can barely walk. How are you going to walk a dog? A racing dog?*

As I struggled to bury Freddie's questions, a flicker of movement behind the woodstove caught my eye. I turned for a more direct look and saw a lanky figure tucked on top of a thick blanket. The shape was partly camouflaged, blending in with the black stove, but I could make out a slender head resting on two front paws. The glint of reflected light in the dog's eyes let me know she was watching me.

"Is that greyhound yours?" I asked.

"No, she's part of the rescued group," Kathy replied. "But she doesn't want to socialize with the others. She's sort of withdrawn. It's like she's depressed. We haven't been able to coax her out of her shell."

"Is she ill?"

"Not ill, but she was abandoned and left in a crate with her muzzle still on. She tried to scrape it off to get food and water, so her mouth got infected. Her teeth were in terrible shape. We had to have several of them removed."

I felt a genuine ache. While the other dogs celebrated their new freedom, this poor animal sat alone, unwilling to join in. What a shame.

With a shake of my head, I returned to the task at hand. "I have one question before I announce a coming-home party," I said, stroking the neck of the fawn-colored girl in front of me. "What's her name?"

Before Kathy could respond, a weight plopped into my lap. My eyes snapped down in surprise. A greyhound had leaped onto the couch beside me and laid her head on my thighs, focusing her gaze on my face. The cinnamon and black striped markings on her sculpted, muscular form made her look like half tiger, half dog.

"I can't believe she just did that!" whispered Kathy.

"Who is this?" I asked.

Kathy stepped toward us but stopped a couple of paces away and softly said, "We call her Comet. This is the one from over by the fire."

My skin popped with goose bumps. A buzzing tickled my ears, and my fingers tingled as I stroked the dog's head. She nestled deeper into my lap but otherwise didn't move.

I was not a novice to the world of dogs. I grew up spending summers on a farm where I worked and played with all sorts of dogs, from shepherds to terriers to the typical Heinz 57 farm mix. Most of my adult life I had kept dogs as pets, and I knew that unless canines were angry or scared, they approached humans in various stages of doggy excitement — sniffing, wagging, smiling, curious and eager to please, always alert to the possibility of a treat. Dog body language was a cinch to read.

Except this time. This dog simply lay still, her eyes focused on mine. She alone knew her reasons. She had analyzed the variables, drawn her own conclusions, and decided to cross the room and quietly place her head in my lap. But in that quiet, a message reverberated: *Hello. I am Comet. I choose you.*

■ ■ ■ ■ ■

PART I

■ ■ ■ ■ ■

1

Fall 1998–Winter 2000 — Nebraska to Arizona
"You think I should retire," I said, slowly repeating Tim's bombshell. "You think I should leave the firm. Is this some kind of joke?" My partners sat stiffly in their high-backed chairs, their faces impassive. With enormous effort, I kept my voice low and controlled. "You might be frustrated with my unorthodox work schedule, but all my files are up-to-date and my cases and revenue are in line with those of every person in this room."

"It's not about any of that," Tim said evenly. "We're tired of wondering if you're okay. We can't plan for the future. We can't anticipate. And because you're squeezing a week's worth of work into the three days you *might* make it into the office, we're frantic about you missing deadlines and committing malpractice. How are we supposed to deal with your cases if suddenly you don't show up anymore?"

"Who said I'm not going to show up?"

"Look, Steve, we don't know what's going on with you. But one thing's certain: you're a physical mess. You can't keep doing what you're doing. You're killing yourself, and we're not willing to risk everything while we wait for the funeral." He glanced around the table and each of my partners nodded.

The office was deserted by the time I left. I rode the elevator down to the parking garage and tottered to my car, still trying to process the news. They can't fire me from my own firm! *Can they?* I clambered into my SUV and merged uncertainly into the traffic on Dodge Street.

The western edge of Omaha quickly faded in my rearview mirror as I headed toward the rural lakeside village where I lived with Freddie and our daughters. The area hadn't changed much since it had been Pawnee hunting ground a hundred years earlier. Majestic eighty-foot cottonwoods, with trunks as big around as a pickup truck, populated the banks of the nearby Platte River. To the west, rolling hills of corn unfurled to the horizon. The drive home had always felt like real-life time travel, and it was my favorite part of the day.

But lately the half-hour commute had

become an hour-long grind, not because of traffic but because my back would spasm if I sat for too long. Each journey was my own private Lewis and Clark expedition — frequent stops with a lot of walking around looking at the ground. Today was no different. After one such break, I slowly straightened and found myself locking eyes with a red-tailed hawk perched high in an ancient hackberry tree across the road. His dark stare looked hungry. Predatory.

"I'm not roadkill yet," I said out loud, returning to the car.

At home, I opened the garage door with the remote. Two blond balls of fur raced to greet me, leaping in circles and yelping, their tails thumping against the car as they spun.

"Sit!" I yelled out the window, desperate to exit. Cody, the golden retriever I had rescued from a puppy mill for the price of a broken shotgun, immediately slammed his haunches flat onto the cool concrete. His daughter, Sandoz, continued her whining, whirling dance and promptly stomped Cody's paw. His low, pointed growl convinced her to sit down next to him. Then both dogs turned to me. Cody's lolling, dripping tongue couldn't hide his smile. In his pale face, whitened by age, his black eyes and nose stood out like coals on a snow-man. Sandoz squirmed and wiggled next to him like a schoolkid who urgently needed permission to use the restroom. "Careful," I warned, and they managed to stay put until I was safely inside the house. But despite myself I, too, was smiling, once again warmed to my core by these friends.

As I sank onto the couch, the dogs lay on the carpet in front of me. As usual, they strategically placed themselves in the exact spot I needed in order to stand and walk away. Escape was impossible without some type of physical contact, which I knew was the point. But today, instead of sighing contentedly and shutting his eyes, Cody studied my face closely, ears perked. No doubt he detected the disgraceful stench of failure.

"What's wrong?" My wife stood in the doorway, her face pinched with concern.

"They kicked me out."

"Oh, Wolfie. *Je suis désolé,*" she said, reverting to her native French. "But you saw this coming. Didn't you?"

"No."

She sat down next to me, taking my hand and lifting it to her cheek. "What choice have you given them? They don't have a clue about how bad you really are, because you

20

won't tell them. And the doctors have been warning you to slow down, anyway." I patted her knee but I couldn't look at her.

In the next few days, I learned that in spite of my denial and avoidance during the past year, Freddie had done some thinking about the inevitable. "The doctors say that you're dramatically worse during the winter months because the cold won't let your body relax. And the nonstop stress of your job doesn't allow your mind to cope. The only way we're going to get through this is if you get away from here during the winter, which will also allow us time to emotionally deal with everything." I was puzzled by the emphasis on the words *we're* and *us*. This spinal condition was my problem, not Freddie's. The whole point of my relentless work schedule had been to shield my wife and daughters from the consequences of my illness.

"We could sell that lot in Arizona," Freddie was saying. A few years back we had bought a parcel of land in Sedona. "We could use the cash to buy a small house there, where you could live for the cold months. You always said you felt a healthy energy flowing through all those red rocks."

I know we discussed money — how could we not have, given the drastic slash in

21

income that was to come? And I hazily recall the paralyzing anxiety we both felt about splitting up. Freddie could not leave her job managing the hospital cardiology unit she had helped establish years earlier. For one thing, she loved it, and for another, she was now the sole breadwinner of our household. She and the girls were my last life preservers, and if I moved to Arizona they'd be twelve hundred miles away. There were tears, lots of tears. But there are two things about that week that remain vividly etched in my mind: the totally overwhelming sense of shame, and the reassuring wetness of my dogs' noses pressed against my palm.

One warm November day, about six weeks after I had been deposited in Sedona, I pulled into the parking lot of Weber's IGA supermarket. I kept these excursions to once a week, since it was getting harder to reach for food and push the shopping cart around. Leaning heavily on my canes, I slowly waddled across the lot. My tortured progress took me in a crooked line toward a small commotion on the nearby sidewalk. I toddled to a stop and straightened to see what all the fuss was about.

A group of people were crowded around a slim blond woman. Edging closer, I saw that she was holding the leash to a dog, and it was the dog that had captured the crowd's attention. Not that the animal seemed to notice. His pose was proud and indifferent — if he wasn't exactly bored by the admiration, he was certainly accustomed to it. He stood about forty inches tall, his head level with the woman's hip. His skull was elongated, tapering to a delicate muzzle. Both ears were perked in the same sideways direction above a small forehead. Outsized almond-shaped eyes serenely surveyed the group. The dog's sleek fur was black with a stippled reddish hue, and his deep chest rose steeply toward a thin, almost dainty abdomen. He was extremely narrow and lean, his ribs visible beneath the fur. Sharply defined muscles popped from his haunches, but his front legs were slender. All four legs ended in large, finely boned paws that sported long toes with thick black nails. The paws were slightly suspended above black pads, creating a distinct athletic appearance, like a basketball player bouncing on the balls of his feet. A slim tail sloped straight down from the dog's rear and ended in a small U slightly above the sidewalk.

"What kind of dog is that?" I asked the woman.

Smiling, she said, "This is Lance. He's a

greyhound. I'm Maggie McCurry."

"Sorry," I stammered, feeling like a recluse who'd forgotten how civilized folk behave. "I'm Steve Wolf. But I go by Wolf. It's nice to meet you."

"You, too," Maggie replied. "Wolf. I'll remember that. Almost everyone around here knows Lance, but very few of them remember my name. I guess Lance is pretty distracting."

Entranced, I extended my hand toward the dog and allowed him to investigate my scent. "Is he always this quiet and laid-back?"

I had never met a greyhound in person. My only knowledge of them came from snippets of television footage I had glanced at while channel surfing. I assumed the breed was a bunch of skinny, hyper racing dogs. And I don't know why, but I was sure they were placed on the intelligence scale next to a bucket of hair. My mental image certainly had not included the amazing specimen standing in front of me.

"In general, greyhounds are calm to the extreme and very sweet. In fact, they're known as the couch potatoes of the dog world," said Maggie. As she talked, Lance leaned into her legs.

"Couch potatoes?" I started to ask another

24

question but realized that Maggie probably preferred to get on with her day. "I must be holding you up."

"No, no. That's all right. I'm involved in greyhound rescue, so I like to tell people about the dogs. These racers have a rough life. At about four months of age, they're placed in a crate. After that, they rarely get any attention except to train or race." Maggie's voice softened and she patted Lance between his ears. "As a result, the racers only know how to act around other greyhounds or their trainers. Most don't know how to play or defend themselves. They don't even know how to climb stairs. They're strangers to the world outside their cages and the track."

"How long are they kept like that?"

"Well, they typically race for only one or two years. If the dogs don't win quickly and often, the owners don't want to spend one more dime on their food or anything else. At that point, they're just an expense that needs to be eliminated. Rescue and adoption groups have been formed to keep the dogs from being killed. We really need people to adopt them."

I instinctively stepped back, sensing a hard sell coming my way. Maggie picked up on it and laughed.

"We'd better get going. So long," she said.

"Right. Bye," I replied lamely.

Lance led Maggie through the parking lot, his muscles flowing and his spine articulating with each step. The languid movements reminded me of a cheetah.

The next day was rainy and cold — not Nebraska cold but chilly enough to keep me inside, immobile, and drowsy from pain medication. The rain pelted the concrete slab outside the sliding glass doors, and gas flames waved in the fireplace. I smiled at the thought of a sleeping greyhound warmed by the heat. *Do they ever miss racing?* I wondered. *Are they truly content being still? Are they strong or incredibly fragile, or both?*

After four months in Sedona I became more accustomed to fending for myself, but I never got used to how long it took me to do everything. When I lived at home, Freddie and the girls had always been quick to pick up items I dropped, and if they weren't around, one of the goldens was happy to help. Because I required two canes to walk, I often needed a hand opening doors or an arm to grasp if I had to climb steps. It was only now, without that help, that I realized how much I had depended on them. I had always thought of myself as the original lone cowboy, the guy everyone else leaned on.

Even answering the phone was a hassle. Freddie and the girls usually called at night, so I was surprised to hear it ring early one February morning. After a hectic search that left me panting, I finally retrieved it.

"Is this Steve Wolf?" asked a female voice.

"It is." I sat down to catch my breath.

"Hi, Steve. My name is Anne. I'm part of the greyhound rescue and adoption effort here in Sedona."

Uh-oh. I had almost forgotten that a few weeks earlier, Maggie had cajoled me into filling out an application to adopt a greyhound. I had run into her and Lance at the IGA again. This time Maggie was fundraising for her rescue group, Wings for Greyhounds. She owned a small plane that she piloted around the Southwest, retrieving greyhounds who were in danger of being disposed of by their owners. She then transported the hounds to foster families. Maggie told me she had recently helped rescue a group of dogs that had been abandoned at the Tucson racetrack. I was so moved by her story that I agreed to fill out the adoption application, but I had no intention of actually bringing a dog home.

"Good news," Anne was now burbling.

"The greyhounds rescued from Tucson were placed with a foster family on a ranch outside Flagstaff. The rescues responded and are successfully socializing."

"Excellent," I mumbled. "Congratulations."

"Thanks!" With a hint of hesitation, Anne continued, "The greys all received veterinary treatment — their teeth were fixed and cleaned, shots brought current, and all were spayed or neutered."

I could tell there was more, but I interrupted, "I really am happy about this, Anne. But I'm not feeling so great. May I call you another time?"

"Oh, I'm sorry. I just wanted you to know."

I cleared my throat and prepared for good-bye. "Wait!" Anne almost shouted. "I also wanted to give you the phone number of the foster parents. You were approved to adopt, and I wanted to give you the first opportunity."

No point in arguing. I jotted down the number and address and got off the phone.

I went back and forth about the whole outlandish idea over the next several weeks. What was I doing? Why would I lead these people on? I didn't need any more hassles in my life, not to mention the fact that if I got a dog, Freddie would feed me to the fish. She had been at me for years about saying yes to every request and taking on too much.

Beneath all the uncertainty was fear. It was natural to be leery of the unknown, of course. How would a new dog fit into our family? What would happen if the greyhound just wouldn't socialize? But those weren't the issues that were making me so anxious. I was mad at myself for being a coward. I was afraid that I was no longer capable of taking care of anyone but myself. I was afraid that I wouldn't be able to cope with complex tasks. I was afraid that pain would keep me from caring for a dog who urgently needed love and attention. More than anything, I was afraid I would fail again.

At the same time, everything I had learned about these racing dogs and their survival tugged at me like spring mud pulling at my boots. I knew that life was revealed mostly in shades of gray, but my upbringing had also taught me that certain issues were black or white, right or wrong. Killing healthy dogs in the prime of their life because they don't make enough money is wrong. When you have the chance to right a wrong, in whatever small or large way, you have a duty to step up and do it. But if that was the source of my conflicted feelings, I could simply volunteer to help with fund-raisers.

My attraction to greyhounds was something much deeper than duty. From the first time I saw Lance, sunlight sparking off his smooth coat while he calmly surveyed the world around him, my gut detected an attitude, a wisdom — an aura, if you will — that was Zen-like. I was left with the impression that Lance did not waste any thought or effort trying to correct the past, because he was too busy enjoying the moment. The softness of his eyes whenever he leaned for comfort against Maggie was proof he had moved on. That Lance could so obviously love a human being after being treated like a piece of meat was profoundly touching.

My head told me one thing, but my heart fought back. One evening, as I sat in my recliner weighing the pros and cons for the hundredth time, I wearily thought, *Oh, to hell with this.* I tossed a sleeping pill into my mouth and took a sip of water to wash it down. For some reason a quote by Henry David Thoreau flashed into my mind: "To be awake is to be alive . . . We must learn to reawaken and keep ourselves awake, not by mechanical aids, but by an infinite expectation of the dawn." That sudden thought

rattled me. It made me realize how desperately I wanted, *needed,* to believe that the
sun would keep coming up every morning.
And I had a very strong hunch that these
greyhounds could help.

"I guess it wouldn't hurt to take a look," I
said to the walls.

2

March 2000 — Arizona

One week later, I found myself sitting on the foster mom's couch, looking into the face of a cinnamon-striped greyhound.

"Comet seems to have made the decision for you," Kathy said. And with that, the greyhound was mine.

If Comet's boldness inside the foster family's house had surprised me, I was equally startled by how willingly she jumped into the back of my SUV. Then I remembered that Maggie had told me racing dogs are transported in trailers. As we left the ranch, Comet remained standing, staring out the windows like a little kid on a school bus.

"I know you're not used to being able to see out," I said, wanting to get her accustomed to the sound of my voice. "But with your long legs, you're going to need to lie down before we start going too fast —

it's easy to lose your balance."

Sure enough, as we rounded a sharp bend in the road, Comet fell down. She immediately jumped to her feet and shot me a hurt look, as if I had just played a mean joke on her. In very short order she lost her balance two more times, jumping up each time, unwilling to stay on the carpeted floor.

I pulled to the shoulder of the road and tried to soothe her. "It's okay, Comet. It'll take some practice before you get the hang of it." I may have sounded relaxed, but I was beginning to sweat. How could I get her to lie down? I wasn't flexible enough to climb around in the backseat and maneuver her into the right position. If I opened the rear hatch, I was afraid she'd bolt past me and be gone. But if I did nothing she was going to get hurt; the road back to Sedona was forty miles of mountainous twists and turns.

Fortunately, I had brought several blankets with me. I limped to the back of the SUV, balancing on one cane with the blankets thrown over my shoulder. Very slowly, I opened the hatch. If I weren't careful, I could lose this dog. Then, as if I needed another test, a truck went blasting past and the wind jerked the hatch door out of my hands, leaving me eye to eye with Comet.

33

"Whoa, girl. It's okay," I said softly. She just stood there looking at me with a touch of amusement. I reached out, petting her head and trying to offer reassurance. By all outward appearances Comet didn't need it, but I sure as heck did.

When my heart stopped pounding I began to gently pull on Comet's front legs, telling her to lie down as I helped her onto the blankets. She resisted, so I massaged her ears for a minute to calm her down. Finally she slid to the floor, and I quietly shut the hatch. Comet comfortably reclined on her blankets during the rest of the trip home.

The sky was growing dark when I finally pulled into my driveway, clipped a leash onto Comet's collar, and coaxed her through the front door. The moment she stepped inside, her long nails clicked sharply against the tile floor and she shot straight up in the air like a frightened cat. *What was that noise!* The dog had never walked on tile before. She scrambled another frantic step and leaped straight up again, looking terrified. Stifling my laughter, I quickly ushered her onto the carpet in the great room, wondering what sort of creature I had adopted.

Exhausted and not knowing what might set her off next, I led Comet to my bedroom, where I had placed a large wire dog cage. Since racers spend most of their life inside crates at the track, I hoped the cage would offer some type of security while providing a familiar place to rest — and this one had a nice soft cushion. Comet dashed for it like a ballplayer sprinting for home plate. I left the cage open but closed the bedroom door so she wouldn't make another shocking discovery while I was asleep. After giving her plenty of food and fresh water, I settled onto my own bed and shut my eyes.

The room was pitch dark when I woke up several hours later. I rolled onto my side, trying to see the clock.

"Holy crap!" I yelled and jerked back. Comet was staring at me from the side of the bed, utterly silent. She appeared to be more curious than afraid. My startled response didn't faze her. Then, without any visible effort, she glided off the floor and onto the bed, barely causing a stir in the mattress. She stood next to me for the briefest moment before simultaneously sliding her front legs forward and folding her back legs under her until she was sitting down. I spent the next half hour talking to her, telling her who I was and explaining the mess she had gotten herself into.

"You would not believe this, Comet, but I

used to be an athlete, too." My spinal degeneration had first been diagnosed when I was sixteen, and supposedly repaired at that time with a fusion. I went on to earn two college sports scholarships, for football and baseball. Back pain had flared up intermittently since then, but I had always managed it with bed rest and willpower. Just two years ago I had been in the best shape of my life. I was even training for a triathlon. Then, during a lunch-hour basketball game at the YMCA, I had stumbled after a ball and couldn't get back up. I had to be carried from the court and taken directly to the hospital. The doctors there informed me, "Your back's a mess. You've got dehydrated discs, bone spurs, and stenosis. And the bone around your old fusion has become deformed." The remedy? There was none. "It can't be fixed. Surgery would only help with part of a very complex problem, if it helped at all." I was forty-three years old.

Comet shifted to her side, stretched out, and shut her eyes. "So that's the story," I murmured as I softly stroked her flank. "To be continued."

During the first few days at my house, Comet encountered many curiosities. The television confounded her. For minutes at a time she would stand directly in front of it, watching the action with tilted head and unblinking eyes. Then she would push at the screen with her nose. Finally, after not receiving so much as a wave from the tiny characters, she abandoned her attempts at communication.

Darkness brought different mysteries. The second night we were home, Comet suddenly rushed from the kitchen into the great room and squeezed behind my recliner. Odd. The next night she did the same thing, and I got a little worried. I sat down in a kitchen chair and called for Comet to join me. She crept out from behind the recliner and stood in the great room staring at me but refused to enter the kitchen. The house had an open plan, with the kitchen's sliding glass doors visible from the great room. I saw her wide eyes repeatedly looking at the glass doors, then back to me. Maybe it was something outside. I went and stood next to her, determined to spot the demon. The darkness of the covered patio had created a shimmering, exaggerated reflection of Comet in the glass, making her think I had another dog in the backyard. I laughed when I saw the reflection, and Comet nudged my leg, letting me know my humor was not appreciated. Properly chagrined, I tickled her ears, saying, "That is scary,

Comet. I'll make her go away by closing the curtains." Problem solved!

Some of Comet's reactions were unlike those of any dog I had known. For instance, my golden retrievers hated it when I left them at home, but Freddie assured me that they moped only until they caught the scent of a new adventure. When I returned, their greeting was a massive celebration primarily because they had forgotten I was gone. Comet took it much harder. She soon realized that when I grabbed the keys from the peg by the garage door, it meant I was leaving. Instantly the sparkle in her eyes would vanish, to be replaced by a lifeless wooden stare that reminded me of one of those deer heads mounted over a fireplace. Her tail would droop between her legs and she would turn and slowly walk off, never once looking back at me, like a prisoner on death row. Maybe she acted that way because when she was left in her crate at the track, she never knew when or if her trainer would return. Eventually she was abandoned. Comet was probably convinced this life would be more of the same. I only hoped she would soon understand that I would always come back, and that her life had truly changed.

■ ■ ■ ■

The adoption application had hinted at many of the unique challenges a new greyhound "parent" might encounter. The dogs' upbringing made them brilliant at racing but stunted in terms of human interaction, sort of like canine aliens. They would require a lot of TLC and would need to be taught social skills that the average pet absorbed by growing up with a family. Greyhounds couldn't be kept in an outdoor kennel, because their low body fat made them extremely sensitive to heat and cold. They needed a place to run on a regular basis. As comprehensive as the application was, however, it didn't spell out the daily trauma of a racer's life, which could have a permanent impact on the hound. I uncovered those details on my own, using the nascent Internet.

My interest was piqued when I spied what I thought was a birthmark inside Comet's right ear. I looked closer, and saw that it was a faint tattoo: 11-8-C. She pulled away from me when I tried to glance at the longer markings in her left ear. Racers are identified by those tattoos, I learned. A dog's registration number is tattooed inside its left ear. The numbers and letters inside its right ear indicate its date of birth and order within the litter. (Comet was born in November 1998, third in the litter.) So for the first two years of her life, Comet didn't have a name, only a number. It was a far cry from pedigreed show dogs with their aristocratic titles.

I was certain that I had seen greyhounds in the Westminster Dog Show, which I watched religiously every year. But it turned out that most greyhounds never enter the mainstream world of families or dog shows. A few are registered with the American Kennel Club (AKC) and compete at events like Westminster. However, the great majority of greyhounds are bred and raised as racers and registered as such with a different organization, the National Greyhound Association (NGA).

What are racers? They are the same greyhound in style, appearance, disposition, and ability as nonracers, but because they are registered as property of the racing industry, they are commonly raised like livestock. Greyhounds are treated more like cattle or hogs in a 4-H project than like beloved family pets. It's true that many racing-dog owners are kind to and admire their greyhounds, in the same way that a rancher is kind to and admires his brood stock. It's just that from birth, racing greyhounds are seen as a commodity: raised, bought, sold, and even slaughtered as the economies of the gambling industry dictate.

In an average seven-puppy litter, only a few are tattooed (by three months) and registered (by eighteen months). In the days before rescue, the dogs that were not registered were presumed dead, destroyed because they were deemed unsuitable for the track. Of the registered greyhounds, some are held for breeding purposes, and the rest enter the racing cycle. It takes only a few races to pick out which dogs have a future as winners and are worth pampering. The "losers" are transported from racetrack to racetrack in tiny cages built into trailers, where they run the risk of dehydration, weight loss, and injury. The only reason the losers are kept around anyway is to give the featured racers bodies to compete against. The trainers spend as little as possible on their upkeep.

The animals that survive the travel are forced to live in wood-and-wire crates at the track. The crates are stacked one on top of another and don't have enough room for many of the larger animals to turn around or to stand with a raised head. Their only creature comfort is the shredded paper on the floor of the cage. Crowding so many dogs into such a small space causes extensive flea, tick, and worm infestations. The greyhounds are often muzzled for the twenty or more hours a day they spend in this spartan confinement. Sometimes they are able to drink, but not to eat, through the muzzle. They are mainly fed cheap "4-D meat" — meat from diseased or destroyed animals, which can't be used for human consumption. Their only exposure to life outside their prison comes when they are released a few times a day to relieve themselves and to train.

Throughout most of their four-thousand-year history as human companions, greyhounds have not been trained to race in a circle competing against other dogs. They were initially bred to run long distances over varied terrain in order to chase down game such as deer, which provided food for their owners. When racing on a short oval track with a lot of other greyhounds after being confined and mistreated, bad things are bound to happen. Hips and legs are shattered. Spines are severed. Brains are scrambled. And dogs are electrocuted by the charged inner rail that operates the bunny lure.

Even if a racer survives these risks, the dog's long-term prospects are grim. Hounds who never place in the money far outnumber the winners, and even the winners will start losing one day. Most of the losers are three years old or younger. Because food and care cost money, no racing kennel wants to keep them around. Since greyhound breeders produce tens of thousands of dogs every year, it's easy to obtain a replacement. The president of the Pensacola Greyhound Association summed up the industry attitude when he said, "That's just a bad part of the business, unfortunately. I compare it to owning a professional sports team. If you have one of your star players who isn't putting out, then you have to make other arrangements."

The "arrangements" are what lie at the end of the road for hundreds of thousands of greyhounds. Some are killed legally by veterinarians hired by the dogs' owners. I suspect that the vast majority of vets would never agree to or condone euthanizing young, healthy dogs, but you can be sure there is someone at every track who has no such qualms.

Then there is another option, known within the industry as "going back to the farm." A man named Robert Rhodes operated one such farm — eighteen acres in rural Alabama where he admitted to shooting thousands of greyhounds during his forty-year career in the racing industry. An aerial photo revealed an estimated three thousand greyhound skeletons scattered around his property. Rhodes, a security guard at a Florida track, said dog owners and trainers had paid him as little as ten dollars per animal to dispose of their greyhounds.

Something similar had happened in Arizona. In 1992 the rotting corpses of 143 racing greyhounds were found after the bodies had been mutilated and scattered in an abandoned citrus orchard. After shooting the dogs, the killers had cut off the tattooed ears, hoping it would prevent them from being identified. Good police work led to the discovery of some of the ears, and an Arizona breeder and kennel owner was convicted for his part in the massacre. He was fined twenty-five thousand dollars, sentenced to thirty days in jail, given eighteen months probation, and ordered to perform four hundred hours of community service. Compare that to the punishment of Michael Vick, the professional football player who in 2007 was convicted of animal cruelty and served a twenty-three-month prison term for his part in a dog-fighting ring that resulted in the deaths of several pit bulls. The disparity in those two sentences may point to how differently "pets" and "livestock" are valued.

In addition to the massacres, there are a multitude of documented cases where greyhounds have simply disappeared. Thousands have been "donated" to medical research, and many more have been transported to other countries. Advocates for the Greyhound Protection League say that twenty-five thousand is a conservative estimate of the yearly number of greyhound killings that occurred during the racing industry's heyday from the mid-1980s to the early 2000s.

"If there's anybody to be indicted here, it's the industry because this is what they're doing to these animals. The misery begins the day they're born. The misery ends when my client gets ahold of them and puts a bullet in their head." That is how Robert Rhodes's attorney attempted to defend his client's actions as late as 2003. The defense was ridiculous, but his observations about the industry were on target. A racing greyhound's misery does begin the day the dog is born. However, owing to growing public awareness, greyhounds are being rescued and adopted in ever increasing numbers. By 2003, eighteen thousand retired racers were being placed with families each year. Unfortunately, that still left seven thousand hounds who were needlessly put to death. While the numbers might be fewer today, the percentages haven't necessarily improved.

Watching Comet asleep at my feet, I tried to erase the image of this gentle creature being raced, abused, starved, and abandoned. I could not predict how well she would adapt to her new world, but I could do my best to ease her into it slowly.

3

April 2000 — Arizona

When I first brought Comet home I had been concerned about getting her socialized, but as it turned out, I was the one who needed lessons. Comet's insatiable curiosity about all sights, sounds, and smells in the neighborhood included every human being we passed on our walks. I had carefully cultivated a self-pitying solitude all these months, returning my neighbors' greetings with a curt nod of my head. Not Comet. She didn't gush over people like the goldens did but instead approached them like a well-mannered foreign diplomat. First she'd observe from a distance, giving the neighbor ample time to size up the elegant dog and her less stylish owner. After a few moments, Comet's curiosity would get the best of her. With that unique greyhound dignity, she would stroll over to the neighbor, her head held high and her eyes so wide and inquisitive that the person would melt on the spot. Within a week I was on a first-name basis with all those neighbors I had so stubbornly avoided.

That was how I met Bill and Jana. Although my backyard adjoined theirs, I had made a point of not engaging in any extended conversations. But shortly after Comet's arrival, while she was gleefully poking her long nose into the dozens of mole tunnels in a nearby vacant lot, Bill called out to me, "Is that your new dog?" I wasn't totally over my pity party, but neither was I rude enough to simply nod and turn away. Who could blame Bill for wanting to meet Comet? It wasn't long before I found myself joining him for a drink and a cigar on his patio and then accepting Bill and Jana's dinner invitations.

I was pleased with the way Comet was settling in, especially after some of the horror stories I had heard about other rescued greyhounds. Some could never adjust to the noise level out in the real world. Like a deaf person whose hearing has been restored for the first time, they were overwhelmed by the onslaught of everyday sounds. In the same way, the background activity of normal life caused some greyhounds to become so anxious that they would regularly try to hide in the dark or run away. Other greys had trouble adapting to different dogs or to children because they didn't understand how to playfully join in.

The most tragic tales involved greyhounds who ran away, not because they wanted to but because they were compelled to. The dogs can spot moving objects up to a half mile away, so if they see a distant cat or squirrel, their chasing instincts — reinforced at the track — immediately kick in. If not restrained by a leash or fence, many greyhounds are gone within seconds, and they don't know to stop until they're thoroughly exhausted. With no remaining energy and no experience finding their way home, the dogs are lost. Even worse, they're not used to traffic and don't understand that cars and trucks are dangerous.

Perhaps Comet had so few problems because of the gradual way she had been acclimated to normal life. She had several months at the ranch, and then I adopted her. Life with me was slow, to put it mildly, and there were no other adults or children around to distract her or complicate our routine. Whatever the reasons, Comet displayed an uncanny ease and graciousness with the neighbors.

What surprised me the most those first

weeks was how little actual training Comet required. I was used to teaching a dog through discipline and commands. *Sit, fetch, come here, lie down, no.* That way the dog learned what you wanted and what behavior was expected. In contrast, Comet learned intuitively. She watched how people, especially me, talked and acted. After several days, I realized to my astonishment that she was doing most of this observation while I thought she was asleep. A greyhound's speed requires an incredible amount of energy that must be available at a moment's notice. Greys are not endurance runners who rely on fat for extra stores of fuel. The only way to ensure that the energy will be there when they need it is for the dogs to rest when they're not running.

But resting is not sleeping. Within just a few days of surreptitiously listening to my phone calls and hearing me talk to friends and neighbors, Comet could detect what mood I was in by the tone of my voice. When we were on a walk and I said, "Slow down," she could tell whether I was amused by her excitement or in pain from exertion. If I was in pain, she would wait and patiently walk by my side. Comet's tranquil demeanor was a welcome change from the boisterous goldens and their sweet but exhausting need for attention. She was always alert, even when resting, yet she rarely barked. I was starting to think she was a cat in a dog's body. It seemed she was always watching me, sizing me up as a potential student rather than the other way around.

Just when I would get carried away thinking Comet must be a guru in disguise, able to sense my moods and impart the wisdom of the ages, she would remind me that she was first and foremost a dog. And most dogs are crazy about kids. When Comet met Emily, the red-haired little girl next door, it was love at first sight. The two of them bonded instantly, nuzzling and communing on a private dog/kid wavelength while I dawdled at the other end of the leash. Within days they had struck a deal: Emily and Comet would get together three times a week for an after-school walk. My only role involved paying Emily a stipend.

At the first scheduled walk, I tried to explain to the excited ten-year-old the unique qualities of a retired greyhound.

"Comet is a racing dog — she's been bred to chase things, especially animals that are running away from her."

"Got it."

"If there's a sudden quick movement

51

down the block, she's going to be off like a rocket, so you've got to hold on tight to that leash."

"Got it."

"She doesn't know how to find her way home like other dogs do. She could be lost in an instant."

Emily nodded impatiently. "Can we go now?"

Chuckling, I nodded back. She grabbed the leash from my hand and marched out the front door, calling, "We'll be back in a jiffy."

Her words swirled in Comet's jet stream as the greyhound shot through the open door before Emily got a chance to attach the leash.

"Uh-oh," she whispered.

Comet was gone. I frantically hobbled to the sidewalk shouting her name, and neighbors quickly joined me in a frenzied search. Shouts of "There she is!" and "She went that way!" sailed across backyard fences. But at forty-five miles per hour, "that way" could be Flagstaff in a flash.

An hour later I returned to the house. Flustered and dismayed, I limped through the still-gaping front door, snatched the keys from the kitchen counter, and headed for the garage. I would continue the search in the SUV. It was going to be a long night.

I was just about to leave the room when my vision snagged on a pair of black ears sticking straight up from a sleek triangular head. Comet was outside, peering in through the sliding screen door. Her amused expression asked, *Where have you been?*

That night I sat half dozing in my recliner, bone-tired and intensely relieved that I wasn't out driving around Sedona. Comet lay on the floor in front of me, her rib cage rhythmically stoking her contented fire. Poor Emily had been almost as traumatized by the day as I was. Comet, however, seemed fine.

About two weeks after I brought Comet home, the phone rang just as the sun was dropping behind the nearby cliffs. It was Freddie.

"What's that sound?" she said in response to my hello.

"What sound?" I nervously replied, glancing at the sliding glass doors in the kitchen.

"That noise. It sounds like a barking dog."

"Oh, that. The neighbor's dog is outside. The weather's gorgeous, so I opened the doors."

"What's wrong with your voice?"

I noticed the higher pitch and corrected.

"Might just be some early spring pollen." Grabbing my canes, I hustled across the room to pull the curtains on Comet's reflected twin, which had materialized as the sky darkened.

"So how are you and the girls doing?" I huffed. "Tell me everything."

"Woof woof woof!" Comet barked three quick warnings — totally out of character for her.

"Where are you? That barking sounds like it's in the house." An edge of skepticism crept into Freddie's voice.

"The neighbor's dog. He's standing by my door," I stammered.

"Which neighbor?"

My mind went blank. I had only known the neighbors' names for a week, and I couldn't recall a single one of them now.

"Steve?" *Wolfie* was Freddie's preferred name for me. *Steve* was not.

"Steve, are you still there?"

A good trial attorney is a good storyteller. I knew the same skill was not as highly valued in matrimony, but I scrambled for a persuasive tale anyway. No luck.

"Yes, I'm here," I finally admitted. "That was my dog."

"Your what?"

"I have a new dog. There's this greyhound

adoption agency, and —"

"Wait! What? Did you say greyhound? As in 'racing dog'?"

I felt a head softly brush against my leg.

"How long have you had this dog and when were you going to tell me?"

The floodgates burst and I launched into a breathless monologue. I started with Maggie and Lance, proceeded through Flagstaff, and ended at the sliding glass door. "Comet thinks the reflection is some sort of ghost. She hardly ever barks," I concluded hopefully.

I could hear Freddie breathing heavily, trying to stay calm. "But, Wolf, a *greyhound*? How in the world are you going to care for a racing dog? I can't — I just can't even fathom it."

"Comet chose me. What was I supposed to do?"

"How about not going up there in the first place? *C'est vraiment con!* I thought you told me you have a hard time shopping for food and you never even cook yourself a meal. I worry about you all night. Meanwhile, you adopt a racing dog! I've got to go. I'm too pissed off to talk to you now."

Formidable. In French it means terrific, in English it means fearsome. Both described my wife. Twelve years earlier I had met this petite, dark-haired woman while on vacation in Scottsdale, Arizona. In a thick and unrecognizable (to me) accent, she had introduced herself as "Frederique, but most people call me Freddie." She told me that she lived in the United States but had been raised in France. I was entranced by the way Freddie spoke and looked — the warm olive skin, boyishly short haircut, hazel eyes, and quick, startlingly bright smile. She was full of life, ready for any dare. When we exchanged phone numbers and realized that we shared the same Nebraska area code, I could almost hear the swell of an off-screen orchestra.

Freddie and I dated for two years before marrying and moving in together along with our children: my young daughters, Kylie and Lindsey (their mom lived in Omaha and we shared custody), and Freddie's two-year-old girl, Jackie. The five of us settled into the house on the lake where my daughters and I had been living. Despite some initial clashes, we eventually melded into a new family. Freddie was exuberant, smart, and not at all shy. When she was around the girls, she managed to restrain her penchant for swearing. Was cursing a national pastime in her country? If so, I didn't mind. *Merde* sounded so earthy and poetic.

Freddie's boldness was fine when in service of her joie de vivre. It could turn a little rough when she got stressed, and to be fair, things had been stressful for several years. I didn't really blame her for her harsh reaction to Comet. I just needed a little more time to make my case. After several tense conversations, my wife and I struck a compromise. I would not immediately return "the mistake," as Freddie called Comet. In a few weeks Freddie would come to Sedona and meet the greyhound. Only then, if she still thought "the mistake" was a mistake, would I drive Comet back to the foster family.

On a warm April afternoon Freddie arrived via the airport shuttle — a godsend for me, the Phoenix airport being a four-hour round trip from Sedona. She entered the house and set her carry-on inside the door. Several days seemed to pass during the next few moments as Freddie spied Comet, who was sitting stiffly next to the fireplace like a statue from Tut's tomb. The greyhound eyed us cautiously. My wife's face softened infinitesimally as she said, "It is sort of pretty." Then, before I could exploit any potential weakness, Freddie kissed me and said, "Let's talk."

We sat at the kitchen table. Comet moved

toward my chair to lie down. First her slender front legs buckled, and then her haunches sank until her rear made contact with the floor. Her front paws inched forward until her deep chest touched the ground, and finally, when her entire body was stretched out, her head very gently came to rest between her paws, and her large eyes closed. The slow-motion performance always reminded me of an old building being demolished.

"That was different," said Freddie. "Now tell me why she shouldn't go back." Encouraged, I rushed to fill in the details about Maggie, Wings for Greyhounds, and the treatment of retired racers. Freddie was mildly interested in the flying taxi service, and her face registered shock when she learned of Comet's condition at the time she was rescued. But she zeroed in on the foster family ranch, interrupting my story to point out, "So the greyhounds actually have a perfect home on that ranch, with lots of room to run, which is what they like to do."

"But it's only temporary," I objected. "The family can't keep all the dogs they foster."

Freddie sighed and got up, heading for the bedroom. I followed. Spring sunlight warmed the pillows. Comet trotted in after us and, with a flicker of movement, leaped onto the bed and stretched out. Eyes closed, body relaxed, her pose signaled snobbish disinterest in our guest.

Freddie sat on the bed and reached for Comet's face. The greyhound's liquid eyes snapped open and she glared at Freddie with an expression of hurt and confusion. A loud, low-pitched growl curled in Comet's throat. Freddie instantly jumped up. "What just happened?"

"No, Comet," I said in a stern tone. I walked to the bed, gently pushed Comet onto her back, and stroked her belly. In the same firm voice I repeated, "No," several more times. I was well aware that dogs are hierarchical animals who vie for position within the pack. It was essential that Comet accept Freddie as her superior. Comet rolled to her stomach as I sat next to her. She snuggled her body next to mine and tried to bury her cold nose behind my back. Freddie softly asked, "Has she done that before?"

"No. It's just that you weren't part of the original deal. Maybe this is too much too soon."

To Freddie's great credit, she immediately understood. "Poor thing. She's scared, isn't she? Why don't we leave her alone and let her get used to having someone else in the house."

Late that afternoon, Freddie and I sipped wine on the back patio. I caught up on news about the girls and grilled Freddie about the spring arrival of eagles and herons, the number of neighbors' gloves the goldens had picked off the snow over the winter, and the activity on the lake as boats were returned to their lifts. Freddie had questions, too. She asked about the not-so-tidy house, my worsening limp, and my wince whenever I got to my feet. In the growing darkness, the biggest question descended like fog: with my health steadily declining, how was I going to care for myself, much less a greyhound?

As if to lift this blanket of uncertainty, Comet slipped out to the patio and stood about ten feet away from us, proper as a debutante. Her soft eyes regarded us for a brief moment, and then she seemed to make a decision. She glided forward to a quiet stop directly in front of Freddie. Comet stretched to full height and tilted her head forward, her ears angled to the side. Her eyes focused on Freddie's, and she waited. I have witnessed this ritual countless times since, and I am always struck by its intelligence and purpose. The formality of the greeting seems to slow time and relax the person to whom it is directed. It is a near-human gesture, an armless hug.

"I think Comet likes me!" Freddie declared.

Soon after that introduction, my wife informed me that Comet's decision to join the family was a great idea. Freddie also made it clear that my part in this whole venture was highly irresponsible and bordered on lunacy. I was very lucky the end justified the means.

Much too soon, Freddie prepared to return to Omaha. The ladies, new best friends, eagerly anticipated their next meeting. As she waited at the front door for the airport shuttle, Freddie advised Comet, "Be patient with Wolfie." Then, after a pause, "Keep an eye on him for me."

4

May 2000 — Arizona to Nebraska

The shuttle delivered Freddie to my door-step again in the first week of May. During her brief absence, spring had arrived in Sedona. Electric blue rosemary flowers in my front garden buzzed with bees, and the tangy scent of new sage drifted across the yard. Walnut-sized quail chicks waddled in the lacy shadows of a manzanita bush, as momma quail encouraged a quicker pace. A twelve-foot agave stalk bursting with fuzzy yellow nest-shaped blooms towered overhead. Freddie stepped from the van and stood for a moment admiring the desert diorama. She inhaled deeply, then hoisted her luggage from the back of the shuttle and headed for the house. I stood in the shadowed doorway, wishing I could leap to the sidewalk and grab those bags from her hands. While I balanced on my canes, Comet spun in gleeful circles behind me.

"Wolfie! Comet! Hello!" Freddie shouted, laughing as Comet squeezed past me to greet her. It was a scene straight from a Hallmark card, but my only thought was, *Comet's never that excited to see me.*

Yes, I was grumpy. More accurately, I was worried. Freddie had come to drive me and Comet back to Omaha, where we would gather for the summer at the lake house with our three daughters (and now, three dogs). Kylie, soon to be twenty-one and living mostly at college, and Lindsey, who would be a high school senior in the fall, lived and held jobs in Omaha from June through August, but they loved spending weekends at the lake. Jackie was fifteen and still lived at home. According to the master plan, the family would enjoy the same kind of carefree summer we always had in the past. But I had a strong suspicion that my homecoming might be more like a bad high school reunion, the kind where the star athlete returns as a balding blob of middle-aged mediocrity. I couldn't imagine how the girls would react to my bent spine and crooked gait, which were much more pronounced than they had been the last time they saw me. Freddie had carefully avoided discussing my health with them for the eight months I had been gone. The girls had not pressed her for details.

Sedona was safe because people only knew me as the broken-down neighbor who owned Comet. Home was different. I treasured my daughters. I was far from perfect, and they were the first to point out my weaknesses, especially my inability to dress myself tastefully. But before my fall on the basketball court and subsequent decline, I had always tried to be a man they looked up to, their own flawed hero. I wanted to be the man in the poem "He," written by a much younger Lindsey during one of the girls' childhood adventures to my law office:

He is like a sun that brightens up my life
He can always make me smile when I am
    down
He always encourages me to do my best
He loves me for who I am
He is the best man I have ever known
He is my best friend
He is my Dad

I was scared that I would never be He again. I was petrified that my family might decide that their old memories of me were more comforting than a reunion with a disabled shell of a father.

"Did you make sure the neighbors have keys so they can check on the house once in a while?" Freddie's question penetrated the quiet twilight of the backyard where we sat, exhausted, after clearing the cupboards of food and readying the place for my absence.

"Wolf! Anybody home?" My mind slowly bobbed to the surface.

"Sorry. I was just wondering how Comet is going to adjust to the family and how they'll adjust to her." Varying scenarios, none good, had been playing like movie trailers in my head all week. Now we both watched Comet as she nosed through the rocks and shrubs along the fence. Sensing our attention, she glanced up and trotted over to Freddie.

"She's going to do just fine, aren't you, sweetie?" my wife cooed, scratching behind Comet's ears. Freddie beamed at Comet, but looking up at me, her eyes were serious. "I won't lie to you. The girls are acting like you've lost the rest of your mind. They talk about Comet almost as if we're divorced and she's the new young girl-toy who's coming to meet the family. They haven't seen you in a while, and now they have to share you with a new dog that you talk about every time you call. They think the goldens, especially Cody, will be even less enthusiastic."

I'm sure my laugh sounded a little harsh. "Then I don't have anything to worry about, do I?"

It was probably true that I spoke about Comet and greyhounds too often when I called the girls. Because I had no job and few friends in Sedona, I had a chance to observe Comet more closely than I had ever observed another creature, human or canine. Living with her and learning about her background as a racer spurred me to research the breed itself. What I discovered was fascinating.

Greyhounds are the only breed mentioned by name in the Bible. Greyhound cousins appear everywhere throughout history: in myth and scripture, on Roman vases and Greek coins, on the walls of Egyptian tombs and the tapestries of French castles. King Tut kept greyhound-type dogs, as did Cleopatra. Even the gods prized these swift and graceful animals. They were valued in ancient times for the same reason they are today: their astonishing speed and agility.

Greyhounds are sight hounds, meaning that they hunt using vision and speed, not scent. It was the Romans who first taught them to chase hares, primarily for the pleasure of watching the dogs run. They called this formalized hunt "coursing." The point was not to kill the hare; it was really a race between hare and hound. The dogs didn't compete against one another. Around 1500 BCE the first greyhounds arrived in what is now England. By the eleventh century they had found their way into the upper echelons of society — only noblemen were allowed to own and hunt with greyhounds. Five hundred years later, Queen Elizabeth I established official rules for greyhound coursing, which again involved the pursuit of hares and did not pit the dogs against one another. Coursing required not only speed and sharp vision but also intelligence and flexibility. Over the centuries, greyhound owners cultivated those traits in the breed.

"They're the fastest dogs on earth! They've been clocked at forty-five miles per hour," I gushed to Lindsey during one of my calls to her.

"Cheetahs can do sixty-five," she instantly responded. Lindsey, who wanted to become a marine biologist, was no slouch about her animal facts. If I had listened to her tone, I might have noticed the wounded feelings beneath that comeback. The whole time they were growing up, I could recite my daughters' class schedules by heart, as well as their extracurriculars and the first and last names of their friends. Now my wavering health and Comet consumed nearly all of my attention.

The top of Bell Rock was just reflecting the vague eastern light when Freddie and I left Sedona, the few things I was bringing home loosely thrown behind the front seat. Comet was splayed across her bed next to the rear hatch, luxuriating in the bright sunlight that splashed through the window. A CD of Native American music provided the soundtrack as we drove from Arizona through western New Mexico. After a few hours, Freddie glanced in the rearview mirror at the sleeping Comet. "If we weren't stopping for gas, how would we know when she needs to get out to potty?"

A reasonable question. Comet had suffered only one accident — *one!* — since I adopted her, and that happened the day after she arrived at my house. Perhaps confused about where to relieve herself, she had let go on the carpeted space between the master bedroom and the kitchen.

"Hey!" I had shouted, and the poor dog had shut off her flow in midstream. Her long tail slapped down between her legs, and she glared at me in astonishment.

"I'm so sorry, Comet," I had whispered as I stroked her back. "Let me get the leash and we'll spend some time outside." From that day forward, Comet informed me of her need for a bathroom break by standing directly in front of me with an intense stare, one ear perked sideways over her head while the other horizontally hovered out in the same direction, all accompanied by a very short high note from the back of her throat.

"She's never been in a car this long, but I assume she'll cry like she always does," I told Freddie as she dodged into the car lanes at a truck stop. After that break, we realized that Comet's bladder would not be an issue. Her pee mileage far exceeded the SUV's gas mileage.

All the way to Albuquerque, earlier summers shimmered in my memory, in contrast to what was sure to be the upcoming disaster movie. The discordant scenes outside the window echoed my internal agitation. Bulky casinos were planted in front of ancient pueblos. The distant Sandia Mountains formed a painterly backdrop to billboards urging teens not to use meth. The theme continued as we turned north onto I-25. Santa Fe, a center of government since the conquistadors, was surrounded by hillsides packed with peach-colored stucco houses. In Denver the Brown Palace Hotel, an eight-story marvel when it opened in 1892, was dwarfed by granite skyscrapers.

Two days of gloomy introspection later, Freddie exited the highway in western Nebraska to give us another break. "Wolfie, you have to get out of your head," she told me. "Paralysis by analysis — isn't that one of your pet peeves?" Her light, teasing tone was betrayed by the tension in her arms and face as she opened the hatch, allowing me to slip a leash onto Comet.

I didn't notice the cool evening air, but it must have been invigorating. The collar had barely encircled Comet's head when she flashed by me like one of her celestial namesakes, snapping the end of the leash in my hand, then spinning like a prairie windmill. I'm convinced she stopped only because she got dizzy. Her eyes had hardly refocused when she took off down an invisible path, following an intriguing scent located somewhere in the bottom of a roadside ditch.

"Hold on, Comet! I can't go down there!" For the first time in two days, the corners of my mouth tugged upward into a smile. Comet's frenzied joy reminded me of how our preteen daughters used to react on family vacations when they found out the motel had a pool. All the eye-rolling boredom and demands to have various sisters placed into foster care magically vanished. If life was still so exciting to Comet that she didn't have time to unpack the emotional baggage from her racing days, I could sure as hell try to emulate her attitude.

Our three-day multistate marathon finally ended at the lake. As we pulled into the driveway, I was struck by the different spring that awaited me here. Instead of blooming succulents and newly leafed mesquite trees, I saw muted shades of brown pierced with the vivid green of young grasses. The prairie bloom of wildflowers had painted a deep blush on the cornfields across the lake. Low gray moisture hovered just above the branches of the cottonwood trees, where tiny buds were shedding the annoying resin that stuck to every exposed surface, especially the soles of shoes.

Familiar signs told me that life had been unfolding for several weeks. Green-winged teal bobbed on a small pond next to the road, and Canada geese had returned to the lake. On a sandbar I spotted two bald eagles snipping at each other over a mutually claimed fish corpse. And when I wrested myself from the SUV, the funk of dead fish and algae freed from a long winter under ice still lingered, mixing with a hint of oily gas smells from boats just placed on their lifts.

I had no sooner shut the SUV's door when a bumping, stumbling mass rounded the corner of the house from the direction of the lake. Cody and Sandoz knew only one greeting — *Damn the torpedoes, full speed ahead!* The two dripping wet balls of wheat-colored fur hurled straight at me as I tried to pull my shoes loose from the cotton-wood resin. I heard Freddie's door slam and she leaped into their path, yelling, "Cody! Stop!"

Cody's butt slid, then stuck to the resiny driveway. Sandoz's brain, always two steps behind her body, got the message a little late. She streaked past Cody, braking and spinning her rear end around my legs like a car sliding on ice, finally coming to a belly flop behind me. Freddie glared and nobody moved.

"Come on, Freddie. No harm, no foul?" I was secretly delighted that the goldens still seemed to think I was Whitey Ford — *early* in his career, when he remained capable of throwing a baseball a country mile.

"Steve, this isn't funny. You've got to teach them to stop running when they get within ten feet of you. We didn't drive all this way just for you to get knocked down and hurt by your own dogs." I nodded as Freddie opened the back hatch to let Comet out.

Comet had observed the manic greeting through the SUV's windows. She now stood in rigid profile, not daring to leave the safety of her sanctuary. Her ears were flattened against her head, and her eyes, stretched wide, darted back and forth as if she were watching a rubber bullet bounce off me, Freddie, and the goldens.

Our Sedona days had consisted of a quiet and uncluttered routine. Most activities involved just the two of us and the neighbors we encountered on our frequent walks. In this unhurried atmosphere, Comet's initial timid reluctance had blossomed into a shy curiosity punctuated with bursts of happy excitement. She developed a quiet confidence as a new world was presented to her in bits and pieces she could easily digest. That genteel pace was a far cry from this frenzied welcome. Comet's stare pleaded with me to provide some relief, some quiet space apart from the merry meltdown.

Freddie turned to the still-unmoving Cody and Sandoz. "Why don't you two go on? Go fetch your ball." Both dogs hesitated. "It's okay. Go on now," she urged them. Two heads tilted and two tongues lolled. Then, as if summoned by Poseidon, father and daughter sped to the lake.

I sat on the back bumper scratching the underside of Comet's belly. "I'll bet you just can't wait to meet the rest of the family."

Freddie and I had married when the girls were ages ten, seven, and four, and for the next ten years we had scrambled to keep up with the shifting moods, alliances, and quirks of three very different daughters. Kylie was my firstborn, blessed with the blond hair and blue eyes of her mother, my ex-wife. Being my precious first child and the family's first grandchild, she was our clan's pampered princess. As the oldest daughter, Kylie took it upon herself to bring a sense of (sometimes unwanted) order to chaotic sisterly activities.

Lindsey, three years younger than Kylie, also had blue eyes and blond hair, which was cut short and gleamed a shade lighter than her sister's. Her long legs put her a good five inches taller than Kylie. Lindsey and I were so close that whenever the clucking members of the flock wanted something, they'd tell her, "You go ask Dad. He won't say no to you." Lindsey had been not quite three years old and strongly attached to me when her mom and I divorced. I always had the feeling that the breakup had caused her to doubt her worth on some deep level.

Jackie, Freddie's daughter, was still in preschool when Freddie and I married. Her large brown puppy eyes and long eyelashes were the envy of every female who met her, and the cuteness factor was enhanced by round eyeglasses that corrected for a lazy eye. As the years passed, she could usually be found outdoors kicking a soccer ball, chasing the dogs, or leaping into the lake.

Merging the families had not been smooth sailing. Kylie and Lindsey lived with their mother in Omaha during the week but also spent a great deal of time with me. Naturally they were reluctant to share their dad with some new woman, especially one who sometimes spoke a different language and wanted to live in their home. Jackie had been raised by Freddie, secure in the world of her one-parent household. At first she didn't take kindly to being supervised by another adult, especially since her father, Freddie's ex, had not been a major part of Jackie's life. Given the young ages of our daughters, we had a hard time convincing some people that combining our families was a wise idea.

Shortly before our February marriage, Freddie and Jackie moved into the lake house. Fortunately for me, Freddie's inventive, occasionally zany approach to life intrigued my daughters, breaking through their initial reservations about this new familial unit. Within weeks, Freddie came up with the idea of turning our traditional Sunday afternoon suppers into a culinary grand tour.

"What would you girls think if we decided to go around the world with our meals?"

Kylie's forehead creased. "What do you mean, around the world?"

"Every Sunday we'll make food that represents a different country. Like corned beef for Ireland, lobster bisque for France, sushi for Japan. You girls can decide which country will be featured and can help me prepare the meal. How does that sound?" Over the hundreds of Sundays that followed, Freddie flambéed, fried, baked, and broiled us around the world several times.

There were hurdles, hurt feelings, and misunderstandings along the way to forging our new family, but the girls adapted to one another much sooner than Freddie and I did to our new parental roles. Many nights we stared at each other with glazed eyes across the deserted dinner table, silently communicating the same doubts — am I a parent, a friend, or just a presence? Over time we eventually found our balance.

It helped that Freddie was a born hostess. "Of course you can have your friends over for the weekend," she always agreed. Whenever neighbors on the lake cruised by, Freddie was the first to accept an invitation to hop aboard, relishing the gossip provided by other boaters. Her attitude sometimes struck me as a little reckless: when I advised her to learn how to swim before she tried to water ski, Freddie just laughed and said, "That's what life jackets are for." But overall her instincts were excellent. As the girls grew older and wanted to boat around by themselves, it was Freddie who excluded me as a passenger. "You taught them how to safely drive the boat. They don't need Dad riding along, telling them to be careful and yelling at the boys to get lost." And if I did happen to express reservations about any of this, I was always admonished, "Get over it, Wolfie. Life is good."

I realized very early on in this arrangement that my most humbling blessing in life would be a daughters-only family. It was a surefire antidote to afflictions such as hubris, chauvinism, and tastelessness, not to mention cigar cravings. While not a total cure (symptoms can persist for decades), it did bevel the edges. Still, as the years passed

I couldn't help but notice that certain gender stereotypes were often based on more than a smidgen of truth. For instance, I knew that females, especially when traveling in packs, were much harder on other females than they were on men. Poor Comet was oblivious to this phenomenon.

The day after Freddie and I arrived at the lake, all three daughters materialized at nearly the same time. Kylie and Lindsey drove in from Omaha, and Jackie returned from one of her interminable sleep-overs. Though it was still only May, the temperature had pushed into the eighties, and the older girls lugged beach bags full of their summer swim gear. Following hugs and kisses, the five of us were standing in the entryway when Comet made her appearance. Maybe it was dog pheromones. Whatever the reason, Comet was suddenly a slick of bait floating on a very still ocean.

"Aren't the purebreds supposed to be gray?"

"Her nose is so long it looks weird."

"She's so skinny! She doesn't look anything like *our* dogs."

"If all they can do is run, how's she going to play with Cody and Sandoz?"

"What good is she if she won't chase tennis balls?"

It was one of the few times the pack's chomping was directed at something Freddie cared about. I didn't count.

"I know what you mean," Freddie said. "When I went to Sedona to see her, I had this vision of a nervous, skinny animal that I was going to send back to the rancher's farm or farmer's ranch or wherever she was from. But Comet is really sweet and I fell in love with her. Don't you think she's pretty?" Comet, eyeing the three sharks, hung back near the fireplace on the far side of the family room.

For once, the goldens' total lack of timing and grace saved the day. An arrival home by any one of the daughters never failed to inspire an epic welcome, and if all three were there, it was best just to get out of the way. Sure enough, twin lumps of fur suddenly stormed into the room like a Keystone SWAT team. Nails scrambled on wood floors as the wriggling masses propelled forward. Sandoz's long, feathery tail slapped a mug I had left on a coffee table — it clattered to the floor as Cody writhed around Lindsey. Sandoz flopped on the floor at Jackie's feet and loudly whined a high-pitched *Well, butter my butt and call me a biscuit, look who's here!* Then, like eels in a mating dance around a spire of coral, the

79

retrievers whirled the irked daughters up the staircase and across the landing that looked down into the family room.

"Are you coming outside with us after we put on our suits?" Kylie called down to us. Her voice had a forced gaiety.

"Absolutely. I really missed you guys and want to catch up on everything."

I was far less confident than I sounded. I had expected that the girls would put Comet through a bit of a hazing, if only to assert their allegiance to their first loves, the goldens. What I hadn't anticipated was the hostile edge to their verbal attack. The face-off that had just occurred carried a not-so-subtle message. The girls were scared. Of me.

During our brief greeting, I caught them surreptitiously staring at me when they thought I wasn't looking. I could almost smell an underlying panic, the type of scent a mink might give off when caught in a steel trap. The shock of seeing me so much worse than when I had left was there in my daughters' wide, uncertain eyes and their stinging reaction to Comet. At least that's what I thought at the time.

The nausea burbling in my stomach as I maneuvered into my swim trunks told me I was as scared as they were. Heart pound-

80

ing, I made my way out to the beach.

"Hey, girls! The sun sure feels great!"

They turned quickly at my greeting, and the collective sorrow in their faces almost made me puke. Whatever calamity they had expected, it must have paled in comparison to the sagging bag of flesh waddling toward them, jabbing his walking sticks into the soft sand. Comet trailed behind me, only adding to the strangeness of the moment for my daughters. To me, Comet's presence was as necessary as the canes I leaned on. She had never known the other Wolf. She was devoted to this one.

Comet was having her own problems adjusting. While I had been worrying about my upcoming family reunion for the entire car trip, Comet had been traveling in trusting, ignorant bliss. Then, all of a sudden — poof! — she was the new kid in the middle of a school year. And as the new kid, she was in for a crash course about the rules, the cliques, and the hierarchy that had developed over all those years.

Comet's education began with Cody and Sandoz the morning after we arrived. Whenever a new dog enters a pack, all roles are up for grabs. Our pack had always consisted of only two dogs, and Cody was the unquestioned leader, not because he was Sandoz's father but because he had an alpha personality. Sandoz was more than happy to be the family baby. My concern was that with the addition of Comet, the battle over territory would last all summer.

Freddie and I had always fed the two goldens at the same time in the same place without any problems. The dogs had their routine down. First, Cody would interrupt Sandoz so that he could eat some of her food, just to make sure she didn't have any extra treats from Freddie or the girls. Sandoz never complained. Then, when Cody left the room, Sandoz was free to finish the leftovers in his dish. Comet, meanwhile, had been taught that life was a constant competition for scarce resources. When other dogs were around her food, the threat level of going hungry was highly elevated — a dog-eat-dog (or at least her food) world.

For the dogs' first group meal, we placed Cody's and Sandoz's bowls near each other on the kitchen floor as usual. Greyhounds, because of their long necks, prefer to eat from an elevated bowl, and Freddie had purchased one before our arrival. We placed that a few feet from the goldens' bowls. Comet had barely reached her food when Cody and Sandoz pushed and shoved each other into the room. Instantly, Comet's neck and back tensed as she turned her body to hide her dish from the other dogs. Cody stared and walked directly over to Comet's heavily muscled rear, which he purposely, aggressively bumped. Comet spun around and snarled at him, exposing what was left of her teeth.

"Wolfie, not an *idée* good," Freddie warned, her voice rising.

Comet's snarl was now a slobbering open-mouthed threat. A low rumble vibrated through Cody, and his snout lifted to show his entire array of much larger teeth.

"I hate this, but they're going to have to work it out sometime," I said. "I'll handle it if they go at each other." But how was I going to do that? Pry them apart with a cane? I started to sweat. Then Cody's bass growl exploded in a thundering roar and he rushed Comet.

"Oh *merde*!" shrieked Freddie.

But almost instantly, the echo of Freddie's scream was the only sound filtering through the room. There was no growling, snarling, or yelping. Comet had simply jumped aside to avoid Cody's body slam. That was it. Cody lowered his square head and sniffed at Comet's dish. Then, without so much as a kernel of food, he went to his bowl to eat.

He was satisfied that Comet and he were going to get along just fine.

Now it was Sandoz's turn. The fur on her back rose into a cockscomb as she stalked toward Comet's food, growling. Comet was totally still, her eyes narrowed. Before I could warn the rough-and-tough cream puff, Comet snapped at the air directly in front of Sandoz's face. With one loud yelp, Sandoz scurried to a safe spot between Freddie's legs. There was now another bowl she could clean out, but only after the skinny new kid was done. Order was established and territories marked. There was never another attempt to revise this new hierarchy. With the rules of engagement firmly in place, Comet was ready for her summer education in lakeside living.

5

June–August 2000 — Nebraska

Prior to that summer, I was pretty sure that the only water Comet had seen was in her drinking bowl. The mirrored, moving surface of the lake was infinitely more puzzling to her than the television had been. She would spend hours standing several feet from the water's edge, staring at her own reflection. The comedic routines of the Cody and Sandoz show were just as baffling to her. Comet had never gotten the chance to romp with other dogs in Sedona because she was always on a leash, as were the dogs we encountered on our walks. And at the foster ranch she had been too traumatized to join in the pack's antics.

Here at the lake I had decided to let Comet roam the property without a leash. It was something I never would have considered but for the fact that our community was essentially an island bordered by the lake, a canal, and some nearby bluffs. If Comet wandered off, she wouldn't get too far. And the dog deserved to run free! Plus I wanted her to learn how to play with the goldens. I would watch her like a hawk to make sure she was safe.

Comet's first hesitant attempt to get closer to the dog action was foiled by the intensity of the fun. She had tiptoed closer to the two goldens, allowing her feet to get a few inches into the water. Closer . . . closer . . . and suddenly a pummeling pile of dog stampeded right over her, crashing her into the cold lake and thoroughly drenching her. Dazed as Wiley Coyote, Comet stumbled to safety, collapsing in the sand next to me. I could practically see stars circling her head.

For the next several days Comet sat in the damp sand beside my chair, maintaining a vigil over the nonstop canine recess. Ears cocked at attention, eyes alert and focused, head tilted in constantly changing degrees, she watched as the goldens retrieved tennis balls, chased ducks, and harassed shallow water fish. Finally she seemed to be satisfied that the shenanigans never devolved into a snarling act of competition and survival but were actually just for fun. Warily at first, and then more persistently, she attempted to join in. Before long she got the hang of it, and the show became a three-dog circus. Comet would feign a frontal attack that Cody would parry with a body slam. Sandoz would come rolling into the fray, all fur and no bite. Bouncing from the pack, Comet would employ a flanking maneuver and bound away in the water like a deer leaping over fences. Again and again, back and forth, battles raged and allegiances shifted.

Dogs, like kids, have endless imagination when it comes to inventing games. The goldens knew that swimming after the ducks was the equivalent of treading water — lots of exercise with no real reward other than keeping your head above water. But if the dogs hid and waited for the ducks to come close, then ran and dived off the end of the dock, the game got a lot more spirited. At a dead run Cody would fling his body far from the dock and land square in the middle of a loudly confused, panicked world of feathers. Sandoz would follow with a quick trot, barely clearing the end of the dock with a belly flop. The first time Comet tried this game, she waited, then in full stride sprinted off the dock expecting to hit a solid surface. Just as her feet touched water, she brought her powerful legs forward and threw them backward to gain purchase for the chase. With a whoosh, she plunged headfirst into the water, surfacing a moment later looking like an aggrieved celebrity who had just been tipped at a dunking booth.

Comet refused to be deterred. She was now a dedicated water dog wannabe. Her version of swimming was not a thing of beauty, but I always marveled at her will-power. With body fat as low as 15 percent, a greyhound could in no way approach the buoyancy of other large dogs blessed with a 35 percent fat ratio. While the goldens paddled the lake at will, Comet inched along, her head barely bobbing above the surface and her front legs churning furiously. She would return to shore with fur plastered to her sides, so obviously discouraged that you could almost see an embarrassed flush on her nose.

I was always relieved when the shipwreck survivor finally washed up on shore, but still, the whole tableau was hilarious! I couldn't let loose the deep belly laugh that demanded to explode — it hurt too much — but my obvious chuckles struck Comet as not appropriately sympathetic. She would turn her head away, visibly ignoring me. Not even Freddie's baby talk ("Oh, little girl, are you okay?") seemed to help. If Freddie talked that way to either of the goldens, they would crawl over white-hot coals to be consoled. Not Comet. Invariably, with a twitch of her hind muscles, she would jet away. Skimming along the water's edge like a windsurfer, she would race the beach for a football field length, corner sharply around a distant fire pit, sprint away from the lake, and disappear into a stand of cottonwoods. Soon we'd hear her feet drumming toward us and she would shoot back in our direction, careen just behind us, and close the oval, only to retrace it several more times. Finally — hot tongue extended, flanks heaving — she'd plunge full speed into the water. I never knew if I was holding my breath because I was awestruck at Comet's spectacular athleticism or because I was waiting for her to surface. One thing was certain, though: even Shakespeare would have had difficulty making a more dramatic point.

Those lightning-fast sprints up the shore left me a little concerned that Comet wouldn't stay within the playground's immediate boundaries. Cody and Sandoz had long ago learned not to run off; besides, the fact that all family activities occurred within a short stretch of sand adjacent to our house reinforced our attempts to keep them from wandering. At any moment one of the girls might decide to go on a boat ride, and as certain as a June thunderstorm, the minute the boat was winched down into the water the goldens would rush to the dock and leap on board. The possibility that they might miss their chance to cruise the lake kept Cody and Sandoz within close range of our house.

Greyhounds, of course, had been bred for centuries to chase distant prey. Comet's keen vision could detect the slightest animal movement within a panorama of other activity. If she wanted, she could cover a quarter of a mile in seconds. And what better place to act like a greyhound than at the lake? An unbroken sand beach stretched the length of the canal adjacent to the main lake. Heavily treed bluffs rose to the west before leveling into fields where white-tailed deer snacked on corn. Thick river vegetation to the east provided ideal habitat for beaver, and visiting flocks of waterfowl floated on the quiet water. Gardens were lost to skittering rabbits by mid-June. It was the type of setting that lured any dog's senses.

One dry, lazy summer day Comet pushed up from the damp depression that she had dug in the warm sand. She stretched like a cat, deceptively nonchalant. Relaxed in the early morning sun, I glanced away to watch the goldens wrestling in the water. With the slightest effort and absolutely no sound, Comet twitched her back leg muscles and streaked down the beach. The silent ease of her departure would have shamed a stealth bomber. Her hind paws dug aggressively into the sand and launched her forward in giant skimming leaps. Within three strides, top speed was engaged, and only a spray of sand defined the path. This time she didn't corner at the fire pit. She just kept going.

I grabbed my canes and pulled myself to my feet. Cursing my carelessness, I waddled to the lake's edge and headed in the direction where she had vanished, hoping to get close enough to soothe her into surrender. I was sure her curiosity would slow the speed of her escape, but I saw no sign of her. I returned home alone, as drenched as if I had been swimming. Frustration exploded as I caned down the walkway. "Damn it!" I shouted to no one. My bent body and shuffling feet prevented me from navigating in a straight line. I stopped to straighten and calculate a more direct path to the house. That's when I spotted her.

The fugitive waited expectantly at the lakeside door. She panted, saliva sliding from an extended tongue, her rib cage rhythmically bellowing for air. Not one ounce of anxiousness was evident. Instead, smiling eyes exuded a still, knowing confidence — not quite a boast, but more of a playful jab: *Don't you remember my first walk with Emily?*

In the early days of our return, George, the security guard for the area, would get phone calls from residents who noticed a striped coyote on the beach. His investigation of our lake's version of a Loch Ness monster introduced him to Comet. By then I knew she had no desire to wander into trouble. "Comet never goes farther than the two-story house at the end of the canal," I told George.

"How dare they call you a coyote," said George, squatting on his haunches to look into Comet's eyes. "I can tell you're very refined."

But weren't greyhounds *supposed* to run away? Weren't these hounds supposed to mindlessly chase any wild animal that moved? Weren't these rescues supposed to be skittish about the post-cage world? Maybe Comet was pleasantly clueless about her own breed's instincts. Even as I quizzed myself, I could feel a faint tickling at the base of my skull telling me that something strange was going on with this dog. Maybe it was the brain marinade of pain and drugs, but I couldn't quite define what I was seeing. It was like air — I could feel that something was there, but I just couldn't touch it.

As Comet became more comfortable with Cody and Sandoz, my daughters became more comfortable with Comet. One June morning, as I made my way down to the lake, I heard shouts of laughter coming from the beach. The goldens were swimming after some ducks while Comet lagged far behind.

"Give her A for effort," I heard Jackie say.

"And F for form," Lindsey added.

But it wasn't long before the girls' giggles about Comet's breaststroke turned to loving favors. To give her a fair shot at retrieving a tennis ball, they'd fake-throw a ball for Cody and Sandoz, then quickly fire the real thing into the water near Comet. When Comet was tired, they would help her dig deeply enough into the sand so that the "poor dog" had a cool place to recover while watching the ongoing festivities. When Cody and Sandoz approached, expecting the same treatment, the girls just patted them and nudged them back to the lake.

It was Comet who permanently cemented these new bonds of friendship late one afternoon. Because dog hair magnetically attracts sand and water, each of the dogs gladly submitted to a rinse and a towel rubdown before reentering the house at the end of the day. Cody and Sandoz unquestioningly allowed any warm body to perform this ritual. But Freddie or I needed to be present for a total toweling-off of Comet. The greyhound's experience with muzzles around her snout had been a nightmare that left scars, literally and figuratively. After I adopted her, it was several weeks before Comet allowed me to so much as place my hand on her snout. She still turned her head away when anyone other than Freddie or I tried to touch her there. It wasn't an aggressive move, but it was pointed enough so that many people were left with the impression that she was afraid of them. A towel over her head or near her face was totally unacceptable.

On this afternoon, the three girls were busy with the dog wash. Freddie had been called into the hospital earlier and had not yet returned. I was not having one of my better days, and it was difficult for me to grip the towels. "One of you is going to have to help Comet. I just can't," I said.

At the beginning of the summer, the girls had been offended when Comet averted her head from them. Then I had explained her past. I gently lifted Comet's ears, displaying the numbered tattoos that still made my stomach lurch a little. The girls' expressions had been solemn as I talked about Comet's early life and how racing greyhounds were routinely mistreated, then abandoned or destroyed. My daughters were now acutely sensitive to Comet's feelings.

"Dad, she's going to have to be a little wet when she comes in. I'm not going to force her to let me dry her head," said Lindsey. The rinsing commenced, shrinking the dogs down to their skin. The girls dried Comet's body but left water dripping from her head and neck. Comet walked over to me, but I couldn't bend down. I tried to drag a towel over her face from an elevated position, but that was useless. Comet turned in frustration. Spying the towels dangling from the line of girls who had just finished with Cody, Comet walked over, shoving her head under the towels and walking through like it was a car wash. Everyone was quiet, afraid of breaking the spell. Almost simulta-neously, all three girls began to rub towels gently over Comet's face. Jackie beamed at me. "I think she really likes us now!" The girls' burbling baby chatter told me that they had fallen for Comet, too.

Although she was now a full-fledged member of the family, it didn't take a Holmes to conclude that Comet's primary focus was on me. The most obvious example was at the lake. Comet had perfected the rules of duck chasing and keep-away and was a spirited and entertaining participant. But even though these games could last for hours, she would bow out long before the activities wound down. After thirty minutes of play, Comet routinely found my chair and rested at my feet. At first I encouraged her to continue with the festivities. "Go ahead. You don't have to babysit me." Invariably, my companion would arch the inside corners of her brows, partially squint her eyes, and stare at me much like an exasperated daughter who questioned my sanity. Instead of rolling her eyes, Comet would slowly lower herself to a haughty resting position.

I thought that maybe her physiology demanded a break. With their low body fat, greyhounds were susceptible to exhaustion when exposed to extreme heat or cold for long periods. At the lake, every summertime movement was smothered by boiled air. By midseason, skin was steamed into a tanned leathery consistency and the goldens' coats were bleached to a dirty white. Even with relief from the cool lake water, maybe the heat was just too much for Comet. But she didn't seem tired as she positioned herself apart from the activity, reserved but not unfriendly. She would lift her head when Freddie and the girls called her to come join the water fights, but she would not budge. She seemed preoccupied, not fatigued.

Because of my declining health, there were days when I couldn't even go sit by the water. If I was trapped inside but not in bed, I usually sat in a recliner near the beach level exit. When I sent Comet outside to play with the other dogs, she would stand by the glass door — muscles taut, ears at attention, eyes unblinking — and sternly demand to be let back in.

"Is this dog becoming codependent?" Kylie asked as she opened the door yet again to let Comet inside.

"You noticed?" I felt slightly embarrassed. "What makes you think it has anything to do with me?"

"Duh," said Kylie. "No matter what she's doing or where she's at, Comet wants to know what *you're* doing and where *you're* at."

"I don't think she's that bad," I replied, perhaps a bit defensively.

"You must feed her a lot of treats. Nobody

wants to spend *that* much time with you," Kylie joked.

"Very funny. I don't give her any treats. Comet has appointed Freddie to that department." I struggled daily to articulate what I observed in this dog. Now I said, "At first I thought it was her reaction to the heat and activity, that maybe she was tired and confused."

Kylie coughed a short laugh and said, "Confused she is not. I'd say that she's made herself right at home, even sleeping in the master's bedroom. 'Smart' may be the word you're looking for."

It didn't take long for Comet to lovingly insinuate herself into almost every aspect of my day. Her constant presence was seldom demanding. It was more like the sound of waves — a shushing that I barely noticed after a while yet found deeply soothing. Except for my morning wake-up call.

I had pigheadedly ignored Freddie's advice that I move my personal headquarters to the bedroom on the lower level, insisting that treading up and down the stairs was good exercise for me and good practice for Comet. Plus, by keeping my sleeping arrangements in the master bedroom on the main floor, I could still pretend that I was adequately soldiering on as a good husband.

During the night, Comet slept on a dog bed within my arm's reach. As dawn approached she would leave her lair, waking me with a light leap onto the bed and an intense stare that poked at me like a stick. Through the open window I would catch the musical notes of dogs splashing along the shore, a lovely sound but not one I needed to hear so early. I'd open my eyes to see my face reflected in cinnamon-rimmed black orbs that sparkled above a pointy-toothed dog smile. An extralong tail rotating in slow circles backstopped the expression. Short, whining trumpet notes were directed at my irritated expression: *It's time to get up, time to get up, time to get up in the morning!*

My response was always in the nature of a cotton-mouthed stutter: "Comet, it's still early. Lie down. We'll go in a minute, okay?"

In return, Comet would lower herself onto the blankets and promptly twist onto her back. One front limb was raised to the ceiling while thighs plopped open. From chest to tail, her tender underside was completely exposed, inviting my light scratching strokes. Her inverted head rubbed on the bed coverings. The belly rubs continued for a few minutes, erasing my reluctance to face the day. "All right, I'll get up."

Magic hovered over the lakeside in the

early morning hours. Nighttime smells lingered, and creatures still mingled at the edge of darkness. Comet's curious ears pricked at rustling sounds in the riparian grasses, and her eyes roamed the shadows for the slightest ghostly movement. The hound nose inventoried each and every scent dropped on wildflowers growing in the sand. All this was conducted with unbridled enthusiasm, as if she had never experienced these sights and smells, much less done so just the day before. After all, something could have changed! I'm convinced Comet pitied my inability to notice.

Regardless of the enticements, Comet would not yank on the lead. She would not sprint ahead to a neck-jerking stop but instead loitered at each scent. She pounced at fleeing rabbits with no forward motion and allowed ducks to swim unimpeded. In short, despite her excitement, Comet refused to instinctively hunt the morning in normal greyhound fashion.

Occasionally I stumbled and tripped to the ground, losing the lead. I was sure Comet would flee, as her ancestral genes ordered her to do. Yet she simply wandered nearby and glanced at me as I strained to lever myself upright. After one such mishap, I grunted, "You're probably just scared, aren't you, girl? That's why you don't take off, isn't it?" Comet answered with a reluctant lift of her nose from an animal hole near a decayed cottonwood stump. *Scared, indeed.*

Then there were the days I was unable to rise at all — sometimes as many as fourteen hours of bedpans and banality before somebody got home to help me up. Despite my regular cursing at fate and the unceasing boredom, interspersed with my screams of pain from spasms, Comet would gently nestle next to me, place her head on my chest, and act as contented as a farm dog on a sunny porch. This was not normal canine behavior. Even more mysteriously, in our unspoken communication I detected wisdom that seemed to say, *It's all right. I understand.*

Then I'd chide myself. *Am I losing my mind? This dog was kept in a cage most of her life. She hasn't had a chance to understand her new surroundings, let alone my stupid situation. She's a dog. Don't try to humanize her, because that's just cruel. Let her be the greyhound she was meant to be!* Yet over those long summer days I couldn't help but feel that by any standard, Comet was far from ordinary.

These jumbled thoughts were emblematic

of all the issues swimming around in my head. I didn't have a job and didn't know if I ever would. How long could we afford two houses? How long would I have to live away from Freddie for part of the year? Would that even work? How could I keep current with the girls? Now that I had spent the summer with them, I was officially up-to-date on their lives — Kylie was looking forward to her third year at the University of Nebraska, Lindsey would be applying to colleges, and Jackie was starting her sophomore year in high school. I asked them questions about their plans, but even as they answered me, I often lost focus, lulled by medications or distracted by an endless mental loop of worry. Once I returned to Arizona, I knew I might once again fall out of touch with them.

Consumed by these fears, I grew more introverted and cranky with each passing week. I was alert enough to notice that my conversations with the girls seemed to peter out after a few sentences but not to ponder the possible reasons. The specter of Lindsey's hero, He, haunted me, yet I never reflected on the words in that childhood ode. Lindsay had spelled out why she revered that man — he made her smile, encouraged her, brightened her day. There was nothing in the poem about being as strong as Tarzan or able to win a triathlon. But I didn't think about that. Instead I obsessed about my failure to live up to my personal code of valor: if I wasn't the mightiest, kindest, smartest, most driven man in all of Nebraska, I was shirking my duties as a husband and father.

The issue wasn't only my health, or the lack of it. My spinal problems had been a splinter in the family body for some time. But in years past, fueled by massive quantities of denial and stubbornness, I had somehow convinced Freddie and the girls that the light in the distance was not an oncoming train. It was this assurance, buttressed by my continued professional successes, that had encouraged them to believe in me. Now nobody knew what to think or say. The whole situation reminded me of an ancient Japanese poem, a copy of which I used to keep in my office:

I have always known
That at last I would
Take this road, but yesterday
I did not know that it would be today.

My daughters were confused. Freddie was scared and frustrated. Every day I was fighting to pull myself out of a sadness that threatened to drown me.

Fortunately, I had my own personal lifeguard. Whenever Comet rested her head on my chest, I felt as if I were lying on a blanket of soft grass in a forest of Ponderosa pines. Every day was a good day for Comet. In her contented presence, I found enough peace to sustain myself through the summer.

■ ■ ■ ■

PART II

■ ■ ■ ■

Part II

6

September 2000 — Arizona

September arrived with all the charm of a turkey vulture. Dark clouds dripped with chilled mist, and a moldy stench hovered above mounds of decomposing leaves. It was time for me to return to Sedona. As Freddie backed the SUV out of the driveway, she said, "Wolfie, you have to promise me one thing. You have to promise that if you get worse, you'll get some help. You can't keep trying to do it all by yourself."

For me, the journey to Arizona was like going to band camp when all I really wanted was to end the summer playing sandlot baseball. Sure, it might have been good for me, but it wasn't nearly what I had in mind. Even in my childish funk, though, I vowed to myself that I would relieve Freddie's stress by finding people to assist me with things like food shopping, cleaning, and keeping healthy.

Freddie stayed in Sedona for a few days to help me settle in. Her smile became increasingly plastic as the time drew near for her to drive back north. The logistics of our separation were more familiar than they had been the previous year, but my health was becoming such an increasingly black hole that its gravity was crushing Freddie's attempts to act unconcerned. I tried to reassure her by repeatedly telling her, "I'll take better care of myself than I have in the past. I'm not going to tough it out. Promise."

In late September, Sedona's clean, dry air brings out a whole new range of vivid details on the surrounding red monuments. It's a season of caressing daytime comfort punctuated by a light cotton-blanket chill at night. Pearly dawns dissolve into deep, flawless sapphire skies. The nights are so clear that the naked eye can spot moonlight sparking off the solar panels of the passing space station. The first time I saw it, I had to check the morning paper to see if the station was losing altitude.

As soon as we returned, Comet eagerly resumed her daily routine, filled with new confidence and a puppylike curiosity that had emerged during her sand-baked summer. Her mood was contagious and I found myself looking forward to our regular walks around the neighborhood. It didn't take long for me to realize that people noticed something different about Comet.

"Hey, Wolf, how're you doing?" My neighbor Bill was leaning against a low stucco wall next to his kitchen garden.

"How are you guys?" I replied, avoiding his question. Jana, stooped out of sight watering her flowers, popped up when she heard my voice. "It's great to have you back in town."

I duck-walked in their direction, two canes stamping the pavement and Comet's leash looped over my right wrist.

"Comet, how have you been?" asked Bill. Excessive tail wagging is a waste of precious energy for a greyhound. Comet stayed glued to my side, but her long tail looped twice in hello.

"We knew you were back when we saw the two of you walking," said Jana. "Why didn't you call?" Again, I let her question hang in the air, choosing to assume it was rhetorical. She continued, "When I saw you I couldn't help noticing how happy Comet seems. Her coat is so shiny! It doesn't look like it has all that nasty dander anymore."

You know you've bonded with a dog when a simple observation makes you swell with

109

parental pride. "She really does look better, doesn't she? She's come a long way from this spring, both physically and mentally."

Jana nodded. "I was telling Bill last night that I would never have believed this kind of dog could be so patient."

My eyes narrowed. "What do you mean?"

"Oh, the way she walks so slowly to stay by your side. I thought they liked to run, so I expected her to drag you down the street. And she watches you so closely when you stop to rest. It looks like Comet's telling you to take your time, that she's in no big hurry."

"I think she takes her time because she investigates every little thing that catches her eye. A lawn ornament at that corner house was moved yesterday, and Comet dragged me into the yard to check it out."

Bill laughed. "Then what about that rabbit this morning? I was sitting at the kitchen table having coffee, watching you two. I thought for sure I was going to have to pick you up off the pavement. But Comet never even hit the end of the leash. She just jumped and spun in those funny circles."

That night I mulled over their comments and had to admit that I was just as surprised as they were. Compared to last year, I now labored longer in the morning before getting out of bed. Comet would simply stretch her lanky body next to mine and wait. My touch on her neck and ears detected no indication of impatience. In fact, an hour or more would sometimes pass and the only movement would be Comet lifting her head from my chest to shift her position. Our walks were slower than ever, but Comet remained pleased, not the least bit anxious. I had taken her nuzzled affection during my frequent stops to be nothing more than boredom. Apparently Jana and Bill had noticed something different.

So did Rindy James, the real estate agent who sold us our original plot of land in Sedona, then helped us sell it and purchase my current abode. Rindy had become a good friend, and she and Comet had formed a mutual admiration society. Soon after we arrived Rindy paid us a welcome-back visit. When Comet saw her at the front door, she sprinted from room to room, barely able to contain herself.

"She looks so happy and healthy, like she's fully adjusted to her new life," Rindy commented. After greeting her long-lost pal and taking a few more victory laps around the house, Comet lay on the carpet with her head next to my slippered feet.

"Does that little girl still walk Comet once

in a while?"

"Emily? Yes, she manages to avoid her homework a few times a week and earn some spending money. She still occasionally leaves the door open before she puts the leash on. But Comet just races up the street and returns after a couple of minutes."

"You're not worried she's going to run away?"

"I did at first, especially after all the 'lost greyhound' stories. But Comet has had plenty of opportunities to bolt. She just keeps coming back. I guess I lucked out with this particular dog." Comet's eyes were closed, but her ears rotated like twin antennae toward whoever was speaking.

"It's more than luck," said Rindy. "The dog obviously adores you. Comet pays attention to you in some strange way, like she knows she has to be careful with you."

"Maybe she knows I need all the help I can get."

My thoughts were not really so flippant. Most people would unquestioningly accept the hazy nature of this mysterious bond, thankful for an enriched life. Not me. Vagueness troubled me, flying as it did in the face of my training and education. *Everything can be quantified. Any experience can be precisely defined.* I suspected that all these people, including me, were engaged in anthropomorphism — projecting our own relationships, experiences, and emotions onto simple canine behavior. Weeks passed and my denials continued, but as the weather grew chillier, Comet's caring attention to me became impossible to ignore.

Cold is a relative term, especially if you were raised on the Great Plains. Still, temperatures in Sedona can rapidly drop into the teens after nightfall, only to climb into the sixties the next day in the ever-present sunshine. That year, winter arrived before Thanksgiving. The seesaw of changing barometric pressures coupled with the drastic temperature variations slammed my painful joints. My feet felt increasingly wooden as the weather cooled. I took more medication, which pickled my last remaining brain cells. Our morning exercise crept toward noon. On days that I struggled, Comet's look conveyed the impression that a leisurely snuggle was exactly the right agenda. At night I was comforted by her warmth at my side. No longer content to be confined to her cushion on the floor, Comet preferred to sleep on the full, soft mattress next to me.

One difficult day, I was still in bed when Jenny, a woman I had hired to clean my house once a week, arrived at around one o'clock. Jenny had a warm and friendly outlook on life, but she brooked no argument when it came to bringing order to my hovel. Viewing the scene from the doorway, Jenny asked Comet to jump from the bed so that she could help me get to the couch. Comet refused, turning her head and staring at the wall.

"I'm just trying to do my job, so don't you act all high-and-mighty," chided Jenny. "I'm not a peasant. Besides, I know you have to go potty, so cut the attitude." Jenny laughed and tried to position Comet's rear-facing left ear alongside the other one, which pointed forward. As she turned her attention to me, her lips pressed in a firm line. "You know, you really could call your neighbors when this happens and I'm not around." Since Jenny also worked at Rindy's house, she had been versed on some of my struggles, including days like today.

"We're doing all right. I was just about to get up anyway."

Sensing my embarrassment, Jenny turned her attention to Comet. In a mock stern voice, she said, "As for you, Miss Royal Highness, I think I'm going to call you Queeny. Now get down. I mean it."

"I don't feel so good," I called out to

Jenny from the living room a few minutes later. The whine of the vacuum cleaner ceased and Jenny turned to where I lay on the couch. "What did you say?" Before I could respond, she frowned. "You don't look too good. Are you feeling okay?"

"I think the pain or the meds, or both, are upsetting my stomach."

"Well, you need to eat more than that piece of toast. I would cook you something, but you don't have anything in the refrigerator."

"You don't have to be my cook, too. I'll be okay. If I don't make it to the store today, I have plenty of canned soup."

Jenny turned back to her chores and remarked, "I hope you feed that dog better than you feed yourself."

Chastened, I allowed the rumble of the vacuum to numb me into a light sleep. Hours later, a watery gurgle and fierce stomach cramps jolted me awake. A blushing coral sky signaled nightfall. Jenny was long departed, but she had left a large plastic bowl on the floor by my head. Drool from my mouth dripped into it, reeking of the stale tuna I had consumed that morning. Nausea suddenly bloomed up from my guts and I weaved toward the bathroom, desperate to spare the carpet. Once there, I commenced a retching that felt like it was erupting from the innermost soul-storing part of my body. Wave after wave, I rode the roller coaster of sickness. I periodically glanced up to see Comet propped on her deep chest, muscled legs tucked in back and hips raised in a posture that looked as if she were somehow elevated above the floor. She remained there throughout the ordeal.

Eventually the storm was spent and the waters calmed. I crawled from the wreckage and landed on the couch. A cold wetness touched my cheek and I opened my eyes. Comet emitted a small cry as her nose touched me again, her concerned affection so obvious that I felt tears trickling from my eyes even as I dropped into a weary sleep.

Overnight, the temperature dipped sharply, and the furnace battled to keep the house at sixty-seven degrees. By morning my muscles were contracted into frigid lumps. My body had expelled everything, including any remnants of pain medication. I was in trouble. More important, I was frantic about Comet. She had not been outside since yesterday afternoon, yet she refused to abandon the floor by my side or utter the slightest sound of protest. I was now endangering a loyal innocent being who had already endured her share of misfortune. Although it was barely 7:00 a.m., I called Rindy.

She arrived within the hour. A chill, not necessarily from the weather, swept into the room with her. Her expression was one of alarm mingled with disgust, as if it was all she could do to keep from shouting, "What's *wrong* with you?" Comet rushed to greet her, and Rindy immediately grabbed the leash from its hook. Without a word, she left with Comet and the door slammed behind them. Angry at the unspoken judgment, I yelled at the empty space, "I'm fine, thank you!"

A short time later an obviously relieved Comet rushed inside and indulged in food and water. Her sides billowed as she calmed from a run.

Rindy removed her coat and shoes. "It really stinks in here," she announced.

I refrained from telling her that the smell of indignation was equally noxious. "I called Jenny and she'll come over later to clean the mess."

Rindy sat in one of the living room chairs. "So you think you had food poisoning? That can be serious. Do you need to go to the doctor?"

"No, I stopped vomiting a couple of hours ago. I hate to bother you any further, but would you mind getting my medicine? It's sitting on the nightstand."

Rindy fetched the bottle and a glass of water. "It's not that I don't want to help," she said. "I'm more than happy to assist whenever I can. But I can't be around all the time. You have to make arrangements with the neighbors to check on you and Comet." As if to fill any space where I might interject, she rushed on, "I also know of several people who exercise dogs. I'm glad you hired Jenny, but you need more support than that."

"I know, I know."

That barrier now breached, a constructive conversation ensued. Rindy sternly reinforced her opinion and provided names of people who could help. Then, in midsentence, she paused and cocked her head. "What is that?"

"What is what?

"That noise. Hear it?"

Sure enough, I detected a soft friction sound, like hands being rubbed together. Then the door banged like a shot had been fired. I sat upright and turned toward the loud crack. Comet was exiting from the bedroom, rear first. Her knotted muscles levered both hind legs toward the ceiling and forced her head to the floor. Her fragile

118

teeth pulled on an object that refused to budge. Then, with an intense tug, Comet popped her dog bed through the door opening and dragged the heavy canvas cushion across the carpet until it came to rest next to the couch.

"That is one determined dog," declared Rindy.

I was weak and fuzzy-headed, but a deep mulelike guffaw rumbled up from my belly. Comet stared at me for a moment and then melted into the bed without any further fuss.

The dog bed was still in the living room when Jenny arrived later that day. "You didn't lift that bed into this room, did you?" She sounded like a highway patrolman asking for license and registration. I related the earlier event and Jenny snorted, "How gullible do you think I am? Who did Queeny convince to put her bed out here right in everybody's way?"

"I'm serious. Comet did it herself."

Jenny stared at Comet doubtfully. Comet stared back. Jenny blinked first. "I told you that dog's smart enough to know what she's doing," she said. Comet remained motionless, as if poured in bronze. To signal that this territorial skirmish was not the entire war, Jenny said on her way to the bathroom, "That bed can stay there until I'm finished, but it goes back into the bedroom and out of the way before I leave."

Comet grunted and looked at me, her brows raised. "Hey, I have nothing to do with this little spat," I whispered, checking to make sure Jenny had not overheard.

Once again, I slumbered through Jenny's departure. When I woke up, the light tinting the walls a soft mauve told me the afternoon wasn't completely exhausted. Before I could call Comet's name to find out where she was, I heard a short rap at the front door. Then a creak, and the door swung open. A young woman with short dark hair hustled into the living room bearing two large sacks of groceries. Pam was a neuromuscular massage therapist whom I had met shortly after moving to Sedona. She had managed to keep me somewhat mobile over the past year. Pre-Comet, I saw Pam only occasionally, but my promise to Freddie that I would take better care of myself had prompted me to schedule weekly in-home sessions with Pam. I didn't know if her expertise extended to intestinal disorders, but I had called her a few hours earlier and related my adventure in canned cuisine. I was hoping that whatever was left of the tuna could be massaged out of muscle tissue.

Pam lugged the groceries through the living room and into the kitchen as I sat up on the couch.

"You're awake. That's a good sign," she said.

Hearing Pam's voice, Comet trudged out from the bedroom where Jenny had banished her earlier. Her slumped shoulders conveyed the attitude of someone on a chain gang. She leaned against Pam's legs.

"You didn't feed her any of that rotten food, did you?" Pam demanded.

"Of course not."

"I know what will make you feel better," Pam cooed to Comet. "Let's go for a walk."

"There's nothing wrong with her! She's just mad because Jenny, the housekeeper, is trying to show Comet that a new sheriff's in town."

Ignoring my explanation, Pam asked, "Have you called your wife?" Pam knew all about my state of forced marital separation. I didn't confide my innermost feelings to her, but under the soothing spell of her massages I had talked about the general situation. "Maybe you should call Freddie while I try to lift Comet's spirits," Pam said as the two of them left the house.

The last thing I wanted to do was talk to my wife. Any news of distress from me caused her to careen like a pinball from alarm to frustration to guilt. This was just food poisoning; I didn't need to upset Freddie.

Pam and Comet soon returned, breathless and exuding good health. "Did you two solve all the world's problems?" I inquired.

"Not all of them." Pam detached the leash and Comet sprinted to me and stopped just inches from my face, pushing her cold wet nose into my cheek, a sloppy but endearing gesture. Then she trotted into the bedroom. It took her less than three minutes to once again drag her big cushion into the living room, placing it next to the couch where I was propped on a pillow. Meanwhile, Pam was heating some chicken soup. The aroma of simmering broth filled the room as she debriefed me on her walk with Comet. "She turned around after one block and practically pulled me back to the house. Now, seeing this" — Pam motioned to the inert body next to me — "I definitely think she's worried about you."

"Hmm," I responded. A few seconds ticked by.

"Well, I guess I'll set up the table for your treatment," Pam finally said. As soon as she did, Comet lay down underneath it.

"I really am sorry I had to drag you all the way over here," I grunted as Pam began her work.

"Would you stop? I told you I have other clients nearby, so it's not an inconvenience."

Facedown, I quieted and concentrated. It took a focused intent to relax knotted muscles so that the gentle treatment could penetrate. New age instrumental music wafted in the background and aided the effort. After an hour she gently placed a towel over me, signaling the end of the massage. "Don't try to leave the table too soon. I'll be out back with Comet."

About twenty minutes later I found Pam sitting on the patio. "I feel much better. I might live," I announced.

"We're all anxiously waiting to find out."

Pam went inside to pack up her table. When she came back out to say her goodbye, she delivered it with a parting shot.

"I know you're familiar with the Americans with Disabilities Act. Have you ever thought about checking into getting a service dog to help you?"

Americans with Disabilities Act? Service dog? Come on! That stuff is for people who are much worse off than I am.

I started to respond, stopped, and then just sat there, too perturbed to speak. Finally Pam said, "All I'm trying to do is subtly suggest that you're getting worse, not better."

"You call that subtle?"

She plowed ahead. "What about Comet? She's intelligent, strong, and calm. And she absolutely fawns over you." Comet stretched and stood up in apparent agreement.

"Let me try a housekeeper first, okay? Anyway, Comet is a rescued racer. She's not designed to be some kind of helper animal."

"Have you asked Comet? Wolf, I have to tell you something. It appears to me that Comet is already helping you in so many ways. You just refuse to notice. That dog is scary smart."

7

October 2000 — Arizona

Ego is a seductive enemy that makes us lie, cheat, and write bad checks. If you were in a room with me that week, you could have almost heard the feathers plump as I stuck out my chest in defiance. Jenny could come clean my house, but I was not about to have my groceries delivered, hire a personal chef, or look for a service dog. The food poisoning had been a onetime setback. I would be just fine on my own. Bring it on!

Comet could certainly smell the manly hormones as she observed my strained efforts around the house. Her serene gaze followed me, or if her eyes were closed, her ears twitched in the direction of whatever clumsy racket I was making. A nervous determination fueled me, in sharp contrast to the greyhound's amused and calm demeanor. As I huffed and puffed, I couldn't escape the feeling that Comet had conducted her own assessment of our situation. She was just waiting for the right moment to give me a stern lecture about slowing down, accepting the moment, and making the most of it. Despite my hunch that Comet might be onto something, I couldn't stop myself from blundering forward.

At 2:45 a.m. on the night after my food-poisoning fiasco, I got up to fetch some Gatorade from the fridge, tripped over the coffee table, and cracked my rib cage on the table's corner. I crashed to the floor and stayed there, in too much pain to move. The morning came. It passed. By midafternoon it still hurt to breathe, and I remained prone in the same spot on the carpet where I had landed the night before. These freak accidents were getting to be a habit.

Comet had once again been locked inside the house all night and half a day. "Go ahead and pee on the carpet, Comet. It can always be cleaned," I urged her. She slowly got to her feet, turned to the wall, and settled back down with her butt facing me. There had always been a keen independence to this greyhound, and it was never more obvious than when I said something that embarrassed her or was just plain wrong. Telling her to pee in the house fell into both categories. My anguish over her predicament made me curse myself out loud.

Nearly twelve hours after my fall, I heard a knock at the front door.

"Come in," I called. No response. I could turn my face just enough to see a shadow framed by the door's stained glass panel. After many long seconds the shadow started to retreat. I took a deep, agonizing breath and yelled, *"Come in!"*

Dan and Charlotte, a retired married couple, lived across the street and were the neighborhood eyes and ears. I had given Dan a key to my house in case of emergencies, and now he stood over me shaking his head as if this was exactly what he had expected.

"I knew something was wrong when your newspaper was still in the driveway," he said.

"Can you let Comet out?" was my instant request.

As the greyhound relieved herself in the proper locale, Dan guided me to the couch and handed me the Gatorade that had escaped in the night.

"Should I take you to the hospital?"

"No, thanks. There's nothing anybody can do about a broken rib. By tomorrow I'll be able to get around again. I've got enough painkillers to get me over the hump."

No more than a week had passed when,

as I was walking Comet on a nearby trail, a desert lizard took a bite out of my big toe (with midwestern hubris I had worn open-toed sandals). The accident tally was now at three. When the skin started to turn black, I went to a podiatrist who prescribed a series of antibiotic injections and said, "If we can't get it under control, we'll have to consider tissue grafts."

Undergoing tissue grafts was a much more pleasant prospect than talking to Freddie, but at this point I knew I had to bring her up to speed. These mishaps were simply bad luck, or so I told myself, but when linked together it sure looked like I wasn't keeping my promise to her. To soften the blow, I began the conversation with a little light humor. "I always knew there was a good reason why I wouldn't let the girls have a pet gerbil. They have teeth."

"Steve, you have to get more help. I mean it! If I have to, I'll quit my job right now and be on the morning plane. Don't make jokes. *C'est pas drôle!*"

Humor had always been my default position when I felt cornered into dealing with my physical woes. It was the only approach I could take, given the way I was raised. My mom and dad both came from large, poor farm families who tilled the glacial soil of

Iowa, the birthplace of John Wayne. My father had learned from his own family that when facing illness or injury, silence was a virtue.

Throughout his youth, Dad's parents fought to overcome the brutal poverty of the Great Depression by selling grain for rock-bottom prices. There was no money to pay for doctors, and health insurance was a fantasy on the order of buying a brand-new tractor. When Dad's mother and many of his eight brothers and sisters suffered severe complications from diabetes, including having limbs amputated, they did not talk about it. When some of them died young from the disease, the family bore the losses without complaint. There wasn't any room in the emotional budget for openly grieving or railing against fate. When my father was diagnosed with diabetes in his midfifties, he carried on the tradition, never expressing fear or discomfort. It was expected that I would do the same. For me to acknowledge vulnerability, even in a self-deprecating joke, was actually an improvement over my father's seamless stoicism.

Freddie knew all about my family history and appreciated my attempts at humor, gallows and otherwise. However, the frustration in her voice as she begged me to get with the program told me that the comedy routine was doomed. But if I couldn't deflect my situation — particularly my physical pain — using denial and jokes, how *was* I supposed to handle it?

Chronic pain does more than hurt. It turns you inward and shrinks your life down to a narrow tunnel of endurance. What makes the effort bearable is the hope that someday you might find relief. But although there were specific causes for much of my pain, it had long ago defied simple treatments. Some of my problems could not be directly connected to a specific anatomical defect or identified on an x-ray. All too often in recent years, my own macho upbringing was echoed by the very experts whose help I sought. *Suck it up, pilgrim!* Some health providers with real medical degrees thought that chronic pain was "all in your head." Bones heal and nerves regenerate. This attitude was always summed up with the phrase, "I don't see anything on the MRI." If it can't be identified and fixed, it doesn't exist.

The more enlightened medical practitioners recognized that injuries and trauma could impact the body in ways that are still not fully understood. Over time, constant severe pain can change the nervous system by affecting peripheral nerves. As it continues, this condition can change the spinal cord and affect different levels of the brain. Years of uncertainty and lack of a concrete treatment can depress a person to the point of contemplating suicide. Even a person like me.

At the time, ending my life seemed like a reasonable plan. The doctors had stated that my problem could not be fixed. If my spine could not be repaired, I could never have my life back. If I couldn't regain my health, Freddie would forever remain the family breadwinner. If I couldn't be the person my daughters had grown to know and love, what was the point of going on? None. Within six months of being fired from my law firm, I had seen the logic of cashing in on my life insurance policy. It made total sense. Without hope, nothing else did.

A war between my emotions and what passed for rational thought raged every minute of every day. Just when I would conclude that I was a born coward and grant myself permission to pull the plug, genes that had been passed on for generations would taunt, "What a baby! You goin' to give up at the first sign of trouble?" That was always countered with a more studied argument. "You should at least leave your family with financial stability." Detached, I would watch the drama play out at a distance. Every once in a while Freddie would telepathically detect something in the air, repeatedly calling me from work. "You aren't acting right. You aren't thinking of doing something stupid, are you?"

"What are you talking about? Of course I won't do anything stupid. What do you think I am, crazy?" With that, I would hustle back to the mental movie, sitting on the edge of my seat, wondering what the outcome would be.

By the time I moved to Sedona, I had already been in significant constant pain for three full years. I was continually juggling medications in search of the right cocktail to suppress the burning and cramping. I was furious at myself, my body, my former partners, and the unfairness of it all. I believe one reason Comet decided to come home with me that day in Flagstaff was that she knew I needed to cool down. Comet's approach to life was entirely different from what I had been taught. She was not stoically enduring her painful memories, nor was she denying them. She definitely wasn't fuming over them. No dog, not even Comet, would calmly accept a life of cruelty. But to fret about having been born a racing greyhound, riding in cages from track to track, and then being abandoned would have been futile. It would have wasted the time she had left. Comet seemed to understand that.

With Comet more than other dogs, I was always asking myself if I was reading human motives into canine behavior. Yet I am convinced that dogs can think critically and recall past experiences. My daughters once adopted a sheltie named Chip whose former owner, a man, had abused him. Chip was unfailingly loyal to Freddie and the girls, but he wouldn't give me or any other male the time of day. I know that Comet, too, thought about her past. I only had to watch her flinch whenever the breeze from an open window blew an interior house door shut. It wasn't the noise that made her cringe; she wasn't afraid of sound from any other source. It was the memory of kennel doors banging in the wind while she lay abandoned at the Tucson track. Yet Comet was not demoralized or mistrustful. Her gleeful willingness to enjoy her new life was a revelation.

J. M. Barrie, the author of *Peter Pan,* once observed: "The life of every man is a diary in which he means to write one story, and writes another; and his humblest hour is when he compares the volume as it is with what he hoped to make it." Consider me humbled.

It was time to cut the excuses and get moving. I needed help more than a few times a week, and with more than just grocery shopping. A service animal was the only option anyone had suggested, so that was the one I went for. If it meant I had to accept a label I detested — *disabled* — then I would do it. Eight silent days had passed since Freddie and I had spoken, and I had a strong suspicion that the next time we talked, I'd better have something new to say.

The only thing I knew about the Americans with Disabilities Act were those parts that dealt with penalties for discriminating against disabled employees. I had no clue about the provisions that applied to dogs that helped people. In fact, the only "service" dogs I was aware of served as guides for the blind. Those dogs were always Labradors, golden retrievers, or German shepherds.

A little research revealed that in 1990 the ADA had greatly expanded both the category of people needing assistance and, potentially, the type of animal who might provide the help. Disability now encompassed any "mental or physical condition which substantially limits a major life activity." And service animals were not limited to dogs or any particular breed but were now defined as animals who were "individually trained to do work or perform tasks for the benefit of a person with a disability." Dogs who retrieved objects from the floor, pulled wheelchairs, turned on light switches, provided balance, or alerted to seizures and other medical conditions were included, as long as the help was directly related to a disability. Medical facilities, restaurants, grocery stores, hotels, and all other businesses open to the public were required to allow service animals to accompany their "disabled" handlers.

This meant that if I had such an animal, I would be allowed to take him or her with me to all those places, and even onto airplanes. The idea was tempting. It would be nice to have a helper to hold the door open for me while I used my canes. It might hurt less to get out of a chair if there were an assistant to pull me up. And it was awfully embarrassing when a spasm hit in public and I ended up sprawled on the floor or sidewalk. A service dog could provide support when a spasm threw me off balance.

But a greyhound as a service dog? I had

never seen or heard of such a thing. There were good reasons why those other breeds were the dogs of choice. They were big and strong enough to pull a wheelchair but not so large that they couldn't lie next to a restaurant table or on the floor of public transportation. They were smart and had an intense desire to please, which made them easy to train. Most important, they were raised as pets, which meant that they were already socialized and well mannered when they entered the training program.

A rescued racer, in contrast, would seem to be a terrible choice. The typical greyhound spends most of the day resting, which certainly raises a flag about endurance. Greyhounds have little or no desire to please by fetching — it's not an attribute of the breed — and their fragile teeth make the task even more disagreeable. Then there is the potential for getting your arm yanked from its socket if a greyhound spots a cat down the block and decides to give chase.

Yet Comet exhibited all the behavior I had witnessed in exceptional working dogs. She was curious and confident; friendly but properly focused; strong, loyal, and intelligent. The fact that greyhounds seldom bark was an added bonus. And I had reason to believe that far from being genetically inappropriate as service dogs, greyhounds might be ideally suited to the task. My forays into greyhound history had uncovered a quote written by the Greek historian Arrian in 124 AD:

I have myself bred a hound whose eyes are the greyest of grey. A swift, hardworking, courageous, sound-footed dog, and she proves a match at any time for four hares. She is moreover most gentle and kindly affected, and never before had I a dog with such a regard for myself.

That certainly sounded like the greyhound I lived with, and I wasn't alone. Since adopting Comet I had spoken to a number of people in Sedona whom I had spied walking their greyhounds. Determined to learn from these other custodians, I listened carefully as they related stories about their new friends. The retired racers were unusually sweet, calm, and intelligent, the owners reported. However, some of their observations gave me pause. Nearly all of the rescued racers suffered from insecurities as a result of their mistreatment at the dog track. The most common of these were separation anxiety and timid behavior in certain situations, for instance, when it thundered loudly or when public areas became confused and noisy with activity. No matter the hound, though, they all delighted in running — stretching their muscles and exhausting their energy in the exuberant celebration of speed.

It was one of these greyhound owners who told me about a vacant horse arena where I could unleash Comet and let her race to her heart's content. I would stand in the middle of the arena while Comet streaked around the perimeter, as smoothly powerful as a Porsche. She'd do five or six laps, and then without warning she'd rush at me at top speed. At the very last moment she would veer to the side, actually brushing my cane. Then she'd shoot off again as if fired from a slingshot, leaving nothing but the swirling air to wash over me like canine laughter. It was quite a thrill.

I was confident that Comet was exceptionally well adjusted for a retired racer, and she was clearly intelligent. Still, I wasn't an expert on the breed. Maybe it would be wise to call Maggie, who had first introduced me to greyhounds via the regal Lance. For some reason I felt foolish asking her, "Have you ever heard of a greyhound service dog?"

Her warm chuckle made me feel a little better. "No, I've never heard of that. To be honest, I've never even thought of such a thing. But what a wonderful idea."

At least I wasn't a complete fool. "I'm seriously considering it. Are you still flying around the Southwest, saving the greyhound world? How's that going?"

"Not too good," Maggie confessed. "With so many tracks closing, there's a glut of dogs waiting for rescue. Saving them one or two at a time with my plane isn't helping enough. Someone needs to organize a larger effort. Funding some of the bigger rescue groups with money from a real job is probably my best bet right now. I've decided to move to California, sell some real estate, and see what the future holds. Whatever it is, it'll never be as rewarding as rescuing these dogs."

With Maggie's reassurance, the service dog idea began to nag me as persistently as my mom's Yorkie, a nonstop yapper. *I could always check into buying a dog that's already trained. Ah, maybe not. I think three dogs is Freddie's limit. Maybe it's best to give up on such a crazy stunt. Then again . . .* Pam's words bounced around my thoughts: "Have you asked Comet?"

"Comet, what would you think if I asked you for a little help once in a while?" Comet opened her eyes just wide enough to let me

139

know that both of us had already made up our minds.

I started our new adventure by looking at several websites dedicated to service dog training so I could get an idea of how a good candidate behaved. Comet seemed to meet the requirements. She was "clean and healthy," didn't "solicit attention," didn't "vocalize unnecessarily," and didn't "urinate or defecate in inappropriate locations" (unless you were a mole).

There was also a list of minimum training standards. At the top of it: "Must be trained to perform three or more tasks to mitigate the client's disability." Coming up with things I needed help with was not a problem. If it required movement, I probably needed help with it. The challenge was in training a dog to assist with actions usually performed by humans, such as opening doors and helping someone in and out of a chair.

I knew from being around herding dogs that training a canine to perform tasks wasn't as simple as issuing a command to sit or stay. A working dog needed a context: *What is it that you need help with, and how does what you're asking me to do help?* Family pets and farm dogs were well acquainted with human activities. By now Comet was attuned to my daily routines, so I figured she would catch on to my requests fairly quickly. Equally important when it came to service training, family pets and farm dogs craved human approval. Retired racing greyhounds did not. After being raised like livestock, there was only the slightest human-dog connection. Pleasing someone was a concept as foreign as being loved, although the fact that Comet did not run away when she had the chance indicated she might be different. After she pulled her cot from the bedroom to sleep at my side during the food poisoning ordeal, I was certain of her affection for me. For the most part, though, asking a greyhound to help you was like asking a chicken to take a bath. This was not going to be a run-of-the-mill obedience exercise. Maybe I needed a professional trainer.

With help from the Internet, yellow pages, and the local library staff, I cobbled together a list of people who trained assistance dogs and started calling them. My request to have a greyhound trained was met with incredulity at best.

"Greyhounds are too stupid to do anything but run."

"A greyhound? Are you nuts?"

"You might as well try pissing up a rope."

Angry and frustrated, I punched in the number of the last trainer on the list, a man named Charlie. I could swear I heard a muffled snicker when I asked my question, but it was better than the open guffaws of the other trainers. Without much hope, I continued. "If you won't train the dog, can you at least give me some help with the basics, like the standards or process of accreditation or whatever?"

"Pets that just do tricks aren't allowed," Charlie grumbled. "And just because the mutt makes you feel good doesn't count. Therapy dogs aren't service dogs."

"So I've been told ad nauseam." I snapped. "Listen, all I'm trying to do is get some help with stuff I'm having trouble doing." *Stuff!* My language skills were shriveling faster than my muscles.

"Why don't you get a Lab or a regular dog that you know can do the job?"

Despite my annoyance, his gruff delivery made me laugh. "She *is* a regular dog. But I know what you mean. I'm finding out that greyhounds are not the breed of choice."

"You're right about that. But I've gotta tell you, I can't really say why. I've never worked with one. Never had any reason to get away from what I know works. What makes you think this greyhound could be of any use to you?" His growl was still skeptical but not nearly as harsh.

"You mean besides the fact that I absolutely adore her?" A low chuckle vibrated in my ear. "She has a lot of traits in common with some good dogs that I've known before. She doesn't go out of her way to get attention and hardly ever barks. She's calm, even around crowds or loud noises, but she's interested in everything. And because of the track, she's used to being in small places for extended periods of time without whining or going to the bathroom."

"She's good with kids and other people?" He actually sounded curious.

"She'll stand still forever when somebody wants to pet her. And, for whatever reason, she loves little kids."

He continued to question me, and I eagerly provided the answers. Greyhounds are not susceptible to typical canine diseases and rarely have hip dysplasia. While not as stout as retrievers, their large rear leg muscles make for a strong, stable base. I emphasized the incredible patience Comet displayed when riding in the truck or standing on the sidewalk in a crowd. She could go for hours without any type of break, not showing even the slightest anxiety.

Charlie listened for several minutes before

interrupting. "If I didn't know she was a greyhound, I'd say you had a good candidate for training. It's the running after things that'd worry me."

"So, would you train her?" I was hopeful for the first time.

"No, I've got plenty to do without learning a new breed. But give me your address and I'll send you some standards that are out there for the blind and deaf dogs, and a new accreditation process that's being bandied around for service dogs."

I recited my address before he warned, "Now, before you go off on a wild goose chase, you'll save yourself some money if you make sure she has the right disposition. Get her around as many crowds and noises as you can. Test her physically by leaning on her with your weight and pulling back hard on the leash. That'll give you a better idea of her strength. Get her around lots of kids. If she don't bite or kill somebody, you'll be a off to a good start."

I wasn't quite sure he was finished so I didn't respond. "One more thing, make sure you know what it is you want done. Don't waste everybody's time by teaching her things you don't need. It'll help you both understand each other."

"Anything else?"

"Get a regular dog." A loud laugh rolled into my ear just before the click.

And that was it. There wasn't a trainer in all of Arizona willing to risk his or her reputation on a greyhound. The closest I was going to get to professional assistance was the package of information Charlie had offered to send. When that finally sank in, I was left with one option: to train Comet myself. After all, I had trained my share of hunting and herding dogs. I had nothing to lose, plenty of time, and the conviction that if I was up to the challenge, Comet would be, too. I gathered the tools I thought I would need — chew bones and a megasized carton of liver treats — and prepared to launch Comet on her second career.

8

November 2000–January 2001 — Arizona
Teaching a dog new tricks always has its ups and downs. Teaching Comet to assist me was more like being strapped to a series of bottle rockets, each with its own unique explosion. Part of the reason for the combustibility was the list of things I needed help with — nothing on it related to chasing rabbits or hurtling around a track at forty-five miles per hour. Comet would definitely need to acquire a new skill set.

It had taken me a week of close scrutiny to isolate some of my more frustrating activities. After looking at the list, I had the same feeling that hit me when I knew Old Yeller was going to die. Fortunately, by then it was the weekend before Thanksgiving and Freddie was on hand to help me prioritize my needs. She had come down for a brief scouting mission in preparation for the family's visit at Christmas. I could tell that my list of limitations came as a shock to her. After reading it, she gently set it on the table and stared out at the frozen water in the backyard fountain. But in a few moments she collected herself and said, "You need another challenge to take on. I knew this dog would be good for you!" My wife's smile was as relaxed and genuine as I had seen it in a long time. Freddie picked up the list again and took a serious look at it. "I think you should start with the basics, the one or two things you struggle with the most every day."

I had almost four weeks to work with Comet before the family arrived. Heeding my spouse's wise advice, I decided to start with the most basic activity of all, opening doors. The house had lever door handles, which were definitely easier to manipulate than knobs. My challenge was trying to push the lever down with my elbow while grasping my cane for balance. Sometimes my weight would shift too far forward and the door would fly open, launching me onto the floor. Comet hated when that happened; she'd stand nearby with a tucked tail, almost as if she were the one facedown on the carpet. She got tense whenever I had to open a door because she never knew if I would make it through intact. I had tried leaving all the interior doors open, but one or more would inevitably slam shut if I opened a window somewhere else in the house. Comet and I would both jump at the sudden rifle crack of the slamming door. For both of us, being able to open and close doors easily would mean an improved quality of life.

Teaching a dog to push a door open would be easier than teaching her to pull it. "Come here, girl," I called to Comet from the bedroom. After a couple of begging shouts, Comet carefully approached the threshold. I figured that as soon as I shut the door in her face, her desire to be with me coupled with her dislike of closed doors would trigger a desperate need to gain entrance. *I'll just leave her for a few minutes and then crack the door.* It had been my experience with the goldens that the tiniest door opening was an invitation for them to poke their noses through and push their way inside. I was positive I could feel the anxiety increasing from the other side of the door as ten minutes crawled past. I listened intently for any sounds of distress. Comet was always quiet, but I didn't want her to suffer unnecessarily. *Enough!* I finally pulled the door inward a crack, ready to lure her with a few encouraging words. I peeked through the crack. Comet lay sprawled on the sunlit carpet, fast asleep.

All good experiments require a little tinkering in order to eliminate unwanted variables. I just didn't know what the variables were. In Sedona, just like at the lake house, if I was inside or outdoors without her, Comet would stiffly stand at the door, glaring a demand for passage. So why had my trial been met with such indifference? Eventually I realized that Comet was perfectly fine with me alone in another part of the house as long as I couldn't escape to the outside without her.

Enlightened, I took the opportunity the next morning to exit the bedroom while Comet luxuriated in the warm spot I left behind in the sheets. I closed the door and waddled to the kitchen to make a pot of coffee. Comet was trapped in the bedroom, and she knew that I now had access to all of the doors that opened to the outside. She couldn't keep her eye on me if she stayed on the bed with the door closed. My third scoop of beans into the grinder was met with a small cry from the other side of the bedroom door. Five inches of nose and snout emerged as I inched the door open. Not willing to let the teaching opportunity pass, I held a liver snap directly above her black nostrils. Because the door opened toward Comet, her head-wedging attempts were slower than a simple push. But as soon as the opening was wide enough, Comet sprinted through. My smiling anticipation of our reunion was dashed when Comet pompously ignored both the treat and me.

I could see that Comet was upset by the change in our routine. Maybe I needed to issue a command that she would understand as a signal for her to get into training mode. "How about I let you know by saying, 'Time to work'?" Thereafter, I notified the Queen in advance about any training exercises (Jenny's apt nickname had stuck). "Time to work" also became invaluable over the years when I wanted Comet to stop socializing. Amazingly, that's all it took to transform her from a crowd-loving celebrity into a snobby attendant no longer interested in the masses.

I worked with Comet for an hour or two every day on learning to open a door. When Freddie's holiday arrival was still two weeks away, Comet was already short-circuiting my attempts to push the interior house doors open, especially if in helping she could prevent my unannounced exit without her. Most important, I could almost see the pride in her eyes when I said, "Thank you,

Comet." I'd like to take credit for the remainder of her training, but all it took was this lightbulb of understanding to flash: Comet was making it easier for me to navigate around the house, and I was immensely grateful for her help. While gratitude was once a totally foreign concept to Comet, she began responding to my praise like a professional butler, head up and smiling eyes to the front. This understanding was a coal-fired, blacksmith-forged bond of caring that Comet has never broken.

Comet could soon negotiate opening a door like a thief, as long as the latch did not click into the notched slot. Unlike the average dog, who might nudge a door open if it was already ajar and there was something he desired on the other side, Comet would open a closed door and do it at my command. With only days remaining before our surprise holiday presentation for Freddie (who was scheduled to arrive three days before the rest of the family), there was still time to dream up a new experiment. "Let's learn to open the door when the handle is latched."

My inspiration for the training method originated in a visit to our local pet supply store. Because of her sweet disposition, Comet was one of only a few dogs allowed into the small shop. There was always a treat waiting for her, and she could roam the two narrow aisles as she pleased. One pleasantly crisp afternoon, I waited at the counter while the owner wheeled a cart loaded with a forty-pound package of dry kernels and a stack of canned dog food to my SUV. After returning, she began to tabulate the bill. "Do you want me to ring that up, too?" The owner's smile was directed over my shoulder.

"I think I've got everything."

"Almost everything," she hinted. Turning, I discovered Comet lingering two steps behind me holding in her mouth a black and tan, nappy-furred stuffed toy that resembled a baby javelina. *That's what I get for letting her hang around Cody and Sandoz — damn juvenile delinquents!*

"His name is Booda," said the shopkeeper.

Comet spent the rest of that day attacking the javelina and flinging it into the air with her long, muscled neck. It was cute for the first two hundred times.

During ensuing visits, Comet went on to acquire a stuffed animal collection that would have been the envy of any little girl. I finally put a stop to the thefts the day I found a long-armed stuffed blue monkey sitting in the passenger's seat on our drive home. It was that monkey who got the job of teaching Comet how to open doors.

My plan was brilliant in its simplicity, if I do say so myself. I hid all the other stuffed animals in a box in the garage, and then I tightly tied the monkey's long arms around the bedroom door lever. My hope was that when Comet noticed the monkey she would pull at him, thus lowering the lever and opening the door. With no other toys around, boredom would become my ally and the monkey's worst nightmare.

I sat in my recliner, peeking over the top of my newspaper to watch Comet investigate the case of the missing toys. First she poked her nose under and around every piece of furniture. Then she collapsed onto her side in front of the couch, fishing for clues by sweeping her long legs under the frame. It didn't occur to her that she was the only one who could have hidden a toy under the furniture. I could tell her frustration was mounting when I became the object of Comet's classic eye-laser probing. "Why don't we check the bedroom?" I innocently suggested. I carefully opened the door only halfway before Comet followed me in. "Look what I found hanging on the door!"

I love watching Comet calculate her options. A quiet staring tenseness soon morphs into a sparkling glint in her eye, followed closely by *Aha!* as her eyes open wide in anticipation of upcoming fun. In this case, her reaction was much too grand for the room. Comet launched herself up and forward, flying headfirst directly at the pleading monkey. Comet, the monkey, and one side of the double door entry smashed violently forward. Before I could comprehend that the cracking sound was doorway trim giving way, Comet landed and vehemently jerked the whole mess backward, only to launch herself forward again. *This is going to get expensive!* Banging, slamming, twisting, and jerking — in minutes Comet managed to make the monkey a dual amputee, his cotton innards strewn all over the floor. *A new version of manslaughter — monkeyslaughter!* My chortling snorts, interrupted by bursts of hysteria, didn't help as I attempted to free the monkey from the handle before Comet brought the whole door crashing down.

By the time Freddie arrived on the morning of December 22, Comet had a new blue monkey. I allowed her unlimited playtime with her toy in the great room, no door involved, while Freddie prepared her holiday feast. This monkey lasted a whole two days.

Before dawn on Christmas morning, we

154

were rudely awakened by a crashing slam at the bedroom door. *"Mon Dieu!"* yelped Freddie, grabbing at me. I had secretly handcuffed a pink monkey to the lever, but Comet and I had not perfected our act. To say that I leaped from bed would be a stretch, but I did scramble over and pull the stuffed toy from the handle. Freddie instantly caught on. "Oh, Wolfie. You were trying to surprise me, weren't you? You're teaching Comet how to open doors." Her voice, so gentle and sweet, actually caused me to blush.

"Comet, why don't you go play with your monkey in the great room. I'm going to spend some time telling my wife how beautiful she is." I don't think Comet cared that I shut the door behind her.

Freddie, Jackie, my mom, and my sister Debbie's family all convened in Sedona two days later, but Kylie and Lindsey couldn't adjust their holiday schedules to join us. It was my first Christmas without them, and it felt like somebody had bruised my heart with a sledgehammer. The loss wasn't made any easier by my cloudy notion that the girls just didn't want to be around me. I imagined they felt the way I had about my grandma after her leg had been amputated

155

due to diabetes. I was thirteen at the time, in theory old enough to graciously ignore the sight of her empty pant leg. But it totally unnerved me. I couldn't look at it, and I couldn't stop thinking about it. I loved my grandmother and was ashamed of my queasiness. It was easier just to avoid her. Instead of splitting the holiday between me and their mother as they usually did, my daughters had probably decided, "It'd be a lot more fun to spend our entire vacation in Florida with Mom." It hurt like hell, but I could certainly relate.

The family's lack of enthusiasm about Comet's new door-opening skill didn't improve my spirits. I had to keep reminding myself that they thought Comet was just learning a trick, and an unimpressive one at that. My mood lightened at the news that Jackie was going home with my sister, which meant Freddie could stay with me for an extra week.

After the family departed, Freddie delved into an online investigation of service dogs. "Wolfie, did you know that there aren't any certification standards?" I watched her frown at the information on the screen. "From what I can tell, there are only suggestions for how the dogs should behave and what type of assistance is considered proper. I can't see that they need any special tags or vests. About the only thing that can happen is that a business can kick them out if they aren't behaving — barking, running around, bothering people."

"No legal standards at all?" It occurred to me that if one thing went wrong while Comet was in a public space, she would never be allowed back. "I just want to do this the right way. The suggested standards of behavior and minimum requirements specified by the service dog groups make perfect sense to me."

That week I lucked into a new training technique with Comet. Determined to teach her to calmly pull open a levered door handle, I tried attaching her leash before a training session. It worked. For some reason, my holding the leash made Comet focus on the task at hand. By the time Freddie boarded the airport shuttle, Comet was proudly pawing down door levers all over the house. My days of belly flopping into a room were over.

As we waited for the shuttle, Freddie said, "Don't forget about the stuff I ordered for Comet. The vest is bright purple, with 'service dog' stitched on the sides. And the collar and leash are made for handling helper dogs. That way, when you're out in public, people will know she's working." Her words puffed out in frozen clouds. "I'm so proud of you for training her!" A kiss and exhaust fumes were all that was left behind.

It's incredible how a cute cheerleader can motivate a man. After Comet's service vest arrived, I was eager to chart out a course of training that would take us from being window-shoppers to in-store patrons. There were still plenty of tasks I would need to teach Comet around the house, and I had a feeling those tasks would multiply with each passing month. But what really excited me was the prospect of being able to get out in the world again and move around more easily.

I knew I would have to pick training locations carefully. At this time there were very few, if any, assistance dogs in northern Arizona. Most people had never even heard the term *service animal.* The predominant opinion was that if you weren't blind, you couldn't bring a dog into a store. For that reason, I decided that our first exercise should be in the big city, Flagstaff, where the store clerks might be better informed.

Halfway to our destination, I pulled into a rest stop for a trial run. The snow-dusted sand mounds didn't much resemble a gallery-lined street, but Comet didn't care. Drafts of cold, pine-scented air tickled her into a spinning celebration at the end of her new leash. The way she paraded up and down the sidewalk, head raised, signaled that the Queen was pleased with her royal purple vest.

Near the Flagstaff exit I spied a chain discount department store, perfect for our first foray indoors as a team. The short black leash enabled me to keep Comet closer to my side. She had learned to heel within a day. Comet's natural inclination was to walk beside me anyway, so the training was brief. Still, I thought it prudent to maintain a white-knuckled grip on the lead. Comet was not even slightly nervous, entering the store with the same proud strut she had flaunted at the rest stop.

I wasn't exactly shocked when our entrance was met with alarmed glances from the clerks. When they began to stalk our progress, I felt like a water buffalo being surrounded by lions. Comet, meanwhile, decided to impersonate a prairie dog. Standing straight up and balancing on her hind legs, she popped her head above the rows of merchandise and whined at some tantalizing object across the store. Her sudden movement tipped me off balance and I started to topple over. As my slow-motion death spiral unwound, Comet tugged the leash from my hand and scooted away.

"Comet! Come here, girl!" She didn't even glance back but instead glided around the end of the aisle, her eyes pinned on a distant target.

And what was so alluring? A security guard. Not once, not twice, but three times, Comet yanked the leash from my grasp and hightailed it to a side entrance where her prince stood scanning the aisles for shoplifters.

"I'm so sorry!" I said as I approached the guard a final time.

He was kneeling and scratching Comet's ears while she gaped at him like a lovelorn teenager.

"That's why we don't allow dogs in here," he scolded, briefly glancing up at me. The authoritarian tone slid into baby talk as he turned back to Comet. "Although you sure are a polite young thing, aren't you . . . girl or boy?"

Since I seemed to be the only one present who realized that Comet couldn't talk, I introduced her. "This is Comet. She's a female greyhound who's in training to be a service dog." Seeing a total blackout behind the guard's eyes, I motioned to my canes.

160

"She's being trained to help me get around and open doors, things like that."

"Not working out too well, is it? Maybe she's already worked hard enough trying to race. Right, girl?" I blushed deep red and pulled Comet out the door. She dragged at the leash, twisting her neck to gaze back at the guard.

"Why don't you blow him a kiss?" I muttered.

I felt like I had just been kicked out of a basketball game for the rookie mistake of not checking in at the scorer's table. The crowd was jeering and I hadn't even gotten into the game. Fifteen miles down the road back to Sedona, I recovered enough to reflect on Comet's odd behavior. This was the second time she had totally lost her head around a man in uniform. George, our lake security guard, had been on the receiving end of Comet's nudging, tail-wagging flirtation the first time he investigated the fable of the striped coyote. From that day forward, she fawned over him in a way that bordered on disturbing.

Now fragments of a conversation were floating back to me from the ether of all things greyhound. Somewhere I had heard about a racer being saved by a security guard who called a veterinarian after the dog had been deserted at the track. The guard had checked on the hound every night until she was well enough to be rescued. Whether Comet was that dog or not, I firmly believed that such a uniformed man had been kind to her in the past. "Comet, I think there might be a more subdued way of saying thank you." In the rearview mirror I saw her staring out the window, ignoring me. I was all too familiar with that female attitude from my daughters: *What do you know about these things? You're old — and a guy!*

If I was going to be so totally humiliated, there was no reason to go all the way to Flagstaff to do it. The drive had not been kind to me, and I was confined inside for several days afterward. Fortunately, Rindy had given me the name of an energetic neighbor who loved to exercise dogs. Between her and Emily, I now had full coverage for days when I couldn't walk Comet. I had also taken Rindy's advice about having the store deliver groceries. Comet was proving to be a good influence.

As I developed my strategy for our occupation of Sedona, I searched for some legal backup. My goal was to avoid as much confrontation as possible. Comet's service vest should have been enough to reassure people of her higher purpose, but that hadn't been the case in Flagstaff. I scoured the Internet and found that, legally, business owners were allowed to ask whether I had a disability and whether Comet was a service dog. If they asked for details about my handicap or what specific assistance the dog was providing, though, they could be fined. And if someone denied Comet access to the store or told us to leave, well, the Office of the Attorney General had a department dedicated to prosecuting such people. But my profession had taught me that there was a big difference between citing the law and switching on the legal machinery that would force someone to comply. Avoiding conflict was an easier path.

Along those lines, it occurred to me that Comet and I could continue our public training outdoors instead of in a place of business. We could concentrate on stairs, which were always a challenge for me and which Comet did not yet trust. Like other racers, she had not been exposed to steps during her life at the track. At the lake house she had picked her way up and down the stairs to the beach, but she had never really gotten the hang of it. A wide set of outdoor public stairs at a shopping center in Sedona would be an ideal place for us to practice.

We made our first attempt midmorning on a weekday. After a few minutes of fumbling in the parking lot next to the stairs as I attached the vest fasteners at Comet's chest and tummy level, the splendidly attired greyhound emerged from my SUV. Following behind her, I could see she had the preening confidence of a guide escorting a group of tourists through Red Rock country. I let Comet choose her path, her nose leading the way. Eventually she inventoried every scent within reasonable distance and allowed me to lead her to the stairway.

"Whaddaya think?" I was talking to Comet, but my eyes were watching people climbing up and down the stairs. I set both of my walking sticks down on a nearby bench and, with my left hand, gripped the handrail that bisected the wide steps. Cinching the leash around my right hand, I climbed up one step at a time, resting at each interval. During the first few steps, Comet hung behind me like an anchor, only following when I tugged on her leash and clicked my tongue. At each stop, I scratched her chin, reciting what a good girl she was. I had elected not to use one of the metallic clickers the professional trainers prefer because Comet had always reacted so positively to the sound of my voice.

By the time we reached the landing almost halfway to the summit, Comet was negotiating each step in stride with me. Several times I wobbled back and forth like a chainsawed tree about to topple, but I regained my balance by placing my palm on Comet's back. She accepted the weight as a thoroughbred would a jockey's, never once shying away. As we rested, I could hear murmurs from people passing by. "What kind of a dog is that? She's gorgeous! Look at her helping that man. Amazing!" As I regained strength and basked in the reflected praise, my eyes were drawn to the top of the stairs, where a man in white — shoes, sweater, slacks, socks — stood stiffly, a cat nestled in his arms. His glare was fixed on Comet. I gazed directly back at him and continued with our tortured journey to the peak.

"What are you doing here?" the man demanded.

"Do I know you?" I lobbed back.

"I hope not," came the snide reply. "Dogs are not allowed on these premises."

"Who says so?"

"The signs by the entrance, for one! And I'm in charge of this shopping center." Before I could slam home a shot about the

Americans with Disabilities Act, Comet got bored. She strolled up to the kitty, her approach freezing the gentleman to the concrete. Without a drop of malice, she elevated and placed her cold, dripping nose directly on the cat's face. With a scratching, scrambling screech, it leaped from the man's arms and shot into some nearby shrubs. Game, set, match! We left them searching for each other in the tangled undergrowth. Comet and I reveled in our teamwork as we strolled down the walkway that circled back to the parking lot.

With newfound confidence, we began exploring the various Sedona business districts in the weeks that followed. A foam dog bed in the back of the SUV turned it into a posh canine hotel on wheels. Comet was perfectly at peace, patiently waiting to launch into each new adventure. The growing winter throngs in Sedona's Uptown presented an excellent training opportunity, and at first I contented myself with disciplined walks through the jostling crowds. It didn't take long before Comet slowed to match my pace and learned to ignore the menagerie of visiting pets and the occasional stray dog. Her nostrils would quiver (as would mine) at the exquisite scents of burning mesquite and barbecued beef that drifted from the many restaurants, but Comet didn't pull me into any doorways, no matter how tempting.

Wherever we went, being out in public with Comet was like traveling with a rock star. People would gawk, point, do double takes, and approach us to ask the same questions I had asked Maggie about Lance: "What kind of dog is that? Is she always so calm?" I didn't always want to stop and chat, but Comet soon learned that my comment "You can say hi, Comet" was like a page announcing that the Queen would now allow peasants to greet her. She would slowly turn and stand with a fake reluctance as compliments dripped all around her. "She's so soft! Her hair is like rabbit fur. She's so elegant! What sweet eyes." She ate it up like liver treats.

As the weather warmed, the traffic through Uptown increased. More tourists supposedly were always welcome, but many shop owners reacted to the mounting crowds like farmers: when it rained, it was too wet; when it dried, it was too dry. When tourists finally emerged from a winter lull, it was too many, too quickly. Tolerance became as scarce as a real saguaro cactus in Monument Valley (despite all the westerns, they don't grow there).

Aware of the cranky attitude, I practiced outdoors with Comet for several more weeks before feeling bold enough to take her into a local store. I chose an art gallery facing the busy Uptown main street, Highway 89A. I was admiring a bronze sculpture of an adolescent Navajo girl when I heard a choking, coughing sound behind me. I turned to meet the unfriendly gaze of a chubby, nattily dressed middle-aged man.

"Dogs are not welcome in this store." *Here we go again.* I held my ground, and as the man realized that I would not be scurrying from the store, his face slowly turned red. He had set a large painting on the floor beside him, and it was actually vibrating from his touch.

"I'm sorry. I really didn't mean to break any rules, but Comet is in training to be a service dog." I gestured dramatically at the words on her vest. Comet was acting strangely, ears at attention and gleaming eyes conveying something that looked like a challenge. She walked slowly toward the painting and rudely poked her dripping nose right onto the glass, leaving behind a small, slimed signature.

"No. Dogs. Allowed! What part of that don't you two understand?" The sneer was especially unattractive on a face that was

168

now the color of a bad bruise.

"Here's. What. I. Understand." I kept my voice low. "I understand that the U.S. attorney general will not consider your ignorance of the law to be a very good defense." I turned and stomped away. At the door, I pointed my walking stick in the man's direction. "I'll give you a couple of days to talk to an attorney. Then I'll be back for your apology."

On the street I chided Comet, "Gee, if only you hadn't been with me, I could have stayed and talked with the nice man all day!" Fuming, I allowed myself a brief fantasy that had the clerk frantically scrubbing Comet's slime mark off the glass, popping an artery, and keeling over with the painting smashing down on top of him. We hopped into the SUV and searched for greener pastures in a business section a little farther from the tourist crowds. Soon I spotted a gallery situated in a modern stone and glass two-story building. It featured a grand, wide staircase in the middle of the main floor, opening to a bright and colorful upper level.

A youngish blond woman greeted us warmly, in sharp contrast to what we had just encountered. My anger floated away.

"Hi." I extended my hand. "My name is

Wolf. This is Comet."

"I'm Linda Goldenstein. Nice to meet you." She bent over to look into Comet's face without touching her. "A real pleasure to meet you, too, Comet," she said gravely.

"So you don't shoot people who bring dogs in here?"

"Technically the owner doesn't allow pets, but well-mannered dogs aren't a problem. Especially a dog trained to help somebody." Linda was eyeing Comet's vest. Perhaps I wasn't trapped in some kind of time warp after all.

"Maybe you could give seminars to your fellow businessmen." I recapped our recent encounter. "Trust me. In two days, I'm going back there and I'll be expecting a whole new perspective."

"Are you here to see a particular exhibit?" Linda asked.

Little did she know I was entirely ignorant of the southwestern art scene; I had just thought the gallery would be a good training opportunity. "I don't know enough about art to know what I'm looking at. But I'd like to see what you have."

When Freddie visited me, she regularly flipped through magazines about southwestern art. Once she had shown me a portrait of a Native American man that had struck her as especially evocative. I was surprised to see that same painting hanging in the upper floor of the gallery. The image was at once realistic and otherworldly, the saturated colors seeming to shimmer on the surface of the canvas. A shirtless young Indian stared directly at the viewer, his skin faintly glowing, his expression forthright and somehow modern. He was set against a stark white background in which a distant moon hung. His spare headdress — just two feathers — was visually balanced against the moon, and circular tribal tattoos covered his shoulders. Perhaps because of the precise, almost mystical balance of the visual elements, and the frank yet unreadable expression on the young man's face, it was difficult for me to take my eyes off the painting once I started looking at it.

"What do you think?" Linda had walked up behind me, but I was so captivated that I didn't even turn around. "The artist's name is Ben Wright. He's part Cherokee. Ben's work deals with ancient Plains cultures — Crow, Lakota, Cheyenne, and others."

Born in Iowa and living in Nebraska, a man didn't use expressions like *spiritual, moving,* or *engaging,* especially in public. "Wow," was the best I could muster.

I wasn't a player in the art acquisition market, but this day became the genesis of a fascinating education into that world. Over subsequent visits, Linda taught me the basics of emerging and established artists and gave me a primer on art, from furniture to glass to bronze to acrylics. Comet was the Wal-Mart greeter on those occasions, though politely keeping her distance from the other customers until I gave permission to say hello. The gallery's staircase became our training area. Comet's stoic stance while steadying me was a far cry from her former furtive sprints up and down stairways. Fortunately, she showed no interest in any further artistic investigation. The apology that stammered from clerk and owner alike on our return visit to the first gallery seemed to have cured her brief dalliance as an art critic. Still, it was nice to know that my sidekick, like my wife, wasn't shy about finding unique ways to make a point.

9

February–May 2001 — Arizona

All that winter I focused on training Comet. Now that she understood what the goal was, she eagerly absorbed new duties. I taught her to brace me from the front when I got in and out of chairs. If I needed her to, she supported my weight when I walked. She waited patiently in front of automatic doors, allowing me time to get through. When spasms threw me to the floor, she learned to lean down, let me grasp her collar, and pull myself to my knees and up.

Before training Comet as a service dog, I had watched her interact with the various stuffed animals she collected on our shopping trips. When torturing these toys, she used her front paws and feet like a cat, pulling and swatting the animal, then prying it far enough off of the floor with a paw for a firm mouth clinch. It was this dexterity that I had taken advantage of when teaching her

173

to open doors. At first she had mouthed the animal attached to the door lever, pulling it down. By now, though, Comet had learned that it was easier to utilize a front leg and paw to push the lever down like a human.

When I saw how easily Comet thrashed the stuffed animals, I realized that I would have to teach her how to temper her powerful touch. Because greyhounds are tall and lanky, many people assume they're also fragile. Their unusually flexible spine allows them to curl into a sleeping posture (again, like a cat) that takes up far less room than required by most large breeds. But the feline delicacy is all an optical illusion. Greyhounds are not only tall, they're big and strong. People are amazed after examining Comet's spread footprint that it is actually as large or larger than that of most retrievers and labs. And greyhounds make up for lack of fat or body mass with lean, strong, fast-twitching muscle fiber. In fact, greys have a larger heart and a higher percentage of fast-twitch muscle than almost any other breed. Their structural strength, from spine to leg muscles, allows all four feet to be off the ground during each running stride, both when contracted and extended. This double-suspension rotary gallop is the fastest of all canine running gaits. What all this means is that nothing on this dog is dainty or merely decorative, including the neck, which, as I observed, can propel a stuffed animal across a room at warp speed until something solid intervenes.

That was my challenge when it came to teaching Comet a potentially lifesaving skill: fetching a recent addition to our lives, my new cell phone. The first few times I threw the phone across the carpeted room and ordered Comet to fetch it, she tasted the plastic and spat it out like a rancher tasting escargot. I figured I'd solve that problem by tucking the phone inside a stuffed animal — I had plenty of fodder in the box of plush toys I had stashed in the garage. Comet quickly learned that if she brought me the ringing animal on the floor, she'd get a liver treat. The problem was, Comet wasn't a retriever. She didn't "fetch." Instead, she would grasp the monkey-phone in her teeth, retract her long, muscular neck, and fling the thing at rocket speed across the room. Her first phone delivery was via airmail at ninety miles per hour aimed straight at my face. The bruise went away in about a week. After that, I learned to duck during our phone-training sessions. Two broken lamps and a few holes in the drywall were a small price to pay for intact cheekbones.

Eventually I removed the phone from the plush monkey. The only reason I didn't suffer any severe injuries was because Comet had learned to tolerate ringing plastic in her mouth long enough to quickly flip the phone to the floor near my feet, where I could pick it up with a mechanical grabber. Despite her displeasure with the taste, Comet was occasionally spirited enough to bang the cell phone off the solid surface closest to my head. I learned to be judicious in my requests for the phone (only in emergencies!) and with treats. Comet was rewarded only if nothing was broken and no blood was spilled.

In a few short months, Comet learned enough service skills to significantly improve my quality of life. Tasks that used to make me feel pissed off and demoralized became exercises in teamwork — functional choreography that made us both feel immensely satisfied with ourselves. The fact that the training process was often hilarious was a bonus that boosted my endorphins, taking my mind off the reality that with each passing day, I was a little less "able."

The biggest surprise was how our service training transformed my life outside our home. When Comet's magnetic personality was brought into the shops and galleries of

Sedona, my world began to expand in totally unexpected ways. Galleries outnumbered liquor establishments here, something I found astonishing. In the small towns where I grew up, only the churches outnumbered the bars. Linda was my guide to the creative community, introducing me to a host of talented painters, sculptors, and other artists. To me, the gallery scene was as exotic as a trip to Bali. The colors, textures, and even the smells — wood, oil paints, wool fibers, and mineral spirits — tingled my senses and ignited my imagination.

I couldn't believe these were the same places I had driven past countless times, barely registering them as quirky little storefronts. Without Comet, I never would have thought to explore the galleries. It would have been too hard to navigate the spaces without stumbling, and I would have been too self-conscious about my body. With Comet, I opened the doors and we were beckoned inside.

Three weeks after I first met Linda, Comet and I stopped by her gallery to say hello. In a courtyard to the side of the building, I saw a tall, powerfully built man standing in front of a blank canvas that rested on a worn wooden easel. His back was to us, so all I could see was shoulder-length dark hair woven with threads of gray, the straight locks flowing over a white T-shirt tucked into beltless blue jeans.

Linda came to greet us and quietly said, "That's Ben Wright. I've asked him to be an artist in residence this month." She raised her voice and called, "Hey, Ben? Do you have time to meet some friends of mine?" Before he could answer she led us a few steps into the courtyard. On a shelf next to the easel I saw vials of paints and glass jars holding brushes, pencils, scrapers, knives, and other tools. A gentle wave of warm, dry air picked up the scent of mesquite, linseed oil, earth, and a hint of pungent sage. I'm sure that Comet was also absorbing the sounds and smells, but her eyes were focused on the back of the man who stood mutely in front of the canvas.

Just when the silence seemed to be reaching uncomfortable, the artist turned. His face was weathered, but his smile was bright, giving him a youthful look.

"Sorry," he said. "I was just finishing blessing this space with some burning sage." He stuck out his hand to shake mine, clearly assuming that an apology involving sage-smoke blessings was all in a day's work. Just for an instant, I expected him to introduce himself as Gandalf.

Ben was about six foot three and as big-boned and broad-chested as a college tight end. Although he was part Cherokee, his appearance was more Texas Baptist. If ever there was a human who exuded as much calm as a greyhound, it was Ben, and Comet picked up on that immediately. Ben wasn't wearing a uniform, but she forgave him, gliding over to where he stood and leaning her body against his legs. Within five minutes, she had lowered herself into a prone position in a shady spot next to Ben's easel, inviting the work to continue.

Ben accepted Comet's invitation. "Hey, Wolf, why don't you guys stick around and watch me work? Maybe we can both learn something." Thus began sessions that lasted several weeks and immersed me in a world as fascinating as any containing goblins and elves.

"I concentrate on Plains cultures and traditions," Ben told us that first day. "I've personally explored how the ancient teachings are universal and applicable to everybody, all colors, all nations. Like many aboriginal tribes around the world, the Plains Indians believed that everything — every creature, person, insect, star — is connected and interdependent. Life is not to be lived as a pyramid, with man on top and everything else below. These cultures believed that life is a circle, connected to all and ending where it began. So even though I'm part Cherokee, my paintings try to enlighten everybody, spiritually and visually." Ben stopped and grinned at me. "Heavy stuff for an Indian, huh?"

"Yeah, but heavier for someone so white he glows in the dark."

That first afternoon, Ben didn't draw a thing. No painting. No sketches. It was as if he were laying the invisible footings and foundation for a house. How could I not be mystified and excited? While we were in the courtyard, I hadn't thought once about my own situation. I was in the moment for the first time in many months, maybe years. I looked at Comet in the rearview mirror as I drove home. "Art is magic, Comet. And I love magic."

The next time we visited the courtyard studio, I asked Ben, "How do you know what to paint?" He laughed at the bluntness of my question but tried his best to answer it.

"I've been mentally composing for the past few days. This painting I'm working on now" — I double-checked; the canvas was still blank — "is inspired by some passages written by Guru Rinpoche. No, he's not American Indian; he's Buddhist. Anyway, he wrote about how Buddhists think the basic cause of suffering is self or ego, an obsession that keeps a person from knowing the real world. It's a false world if ego is the center of the universe. I'm reading this and seeing the words as a face that has features from different ethnic groups. An indigenous universal man, if you will. I'm going to convey my interpretation of the guru's thoughts by painting that man."

By our next visit, Ben had begun to draw. As he worked, he explained technical aspects of painting — glazing, color mixing, composition, spacing, and other details that completely absorbed me. "I apply several thin layers of clear glaze to all of my paintings because it further highlights the colors and provides depth from the light shimmering over the surface of the canvas," he told me.

Understanding a work of art was like peeling away the layers of earth covering an archaeological site. Each level was only one piece of the final discovery. Just learning about the meaning inherent in one symbol, for instance the medicine wheel, was a lesson containing layers all its own. The wheel designated far more than the four directions. It was like North America's first encyclopedia, containing information about sacred colors and animals, earthly elements, spiritual signposts, and various human races. That was just one symbol. And Ben offered just one artist's perspective. And Sedona was full of artists.

Art became my own version of Buddhism. Because much of the focus was on the understanding and portrayal of others — other cultures, viewpoints, times, and beliefs — it allowed me to remove what I was going through from the center of the universe. My own pain and regret were insignificant when compared with the world as it really was. Living was bigger and better and brighter than any one individual could be. I recalled that the actress Ethel Barrymore had observed something similar about getting outside of yourself: "The more things you love, the more you are interested in, the more you enjoy, the more you are indignant about, the more you have left when anything happens."

On Valentine's Day Freddie came down for a brief visit. Her eyes sparkled when she saw how far Comet and I had come in our training, and I could tell that she was proud of us. Even better, for the first time in much too long I had something fun to share with her. Comet and I escorted Freddie to our favorite galleries and introduced her to Linda and a few other artist friends. The collection of Ben Wright's work at Linda's gallery left an especially strong impression on my wife. Sunday morning, as I began to shave, I saw a small picture of one of Ben's paintings taped to the mirror above my sink.

"I can't get the images out of my head," Freddie confessed. "I know we may not have the money, but I cut that picture out of a magazine just to dream."

"You're right, we can't afford it," I said, but the wheels were already spinning.

I wanted to make a grand gesture. I wanted to inspire something in Freddie besides anxiety. Being parent, breadwinner, supervisor of employees, and the only glue that seemed to be holding the family together was eroding Freddie's normally feisty spirit. That would have been difficult enough without the additional strain of worrying about my emotional and physical well-being. I had the distinct impression that despite her compassion, Freddie was reaching her limit. There was no denying that during our phone calls her remarks had become increasingly clipped and impatient. Being separated most of the year was a burden so heavy that it was obviously stressing the underlying structure of our marriage. Catastrophic failure was a distinct possibility. If I happened to reach one of the girls by phone, their end of the conversation was like a political press statement — brief and devoid of meaningful content. I wanted these incredible ladies to know that my love was constant even if I wasn't.

When Freddie left after Valentine's Day, I called Linda and told her that I wanted to give my wife something that would surprise and delight her and, if possible, pay homage to what was good about our life together. A few conversations later we had concocted a plan that I knew would fit the bill, timed to coincide with Freddie's next visit around Easter.

The evening stars dimmed when I saw Freddie's smile as she emerged from the airport shuttle on the night of the surprise. It would take place after a reception Linda was hosting at the gallery to honor some of the artists whose work was displayed there. Freddie had barely been able to contain herself when I told her about my Art 101 lessons with Ben Wright, and she knew that he would be in attendance that night along with many other artists. After the gallery reception, a group of about thirty of us met at a nearby restaurant, where Freddie and I were seated at a table with Ben, Linda, and a few other artists. Enjoying a fine meal in the company of creative minds was an experience completely at odds with the hundreds of law and medical gatherings we had attended in the past. These people saw the world differently. The discussion didn't revolve around politics or local gossip; instead, they reported on a unique color spotted in the diffuse light at the base of a canyon, or laughed about how conversations were similar to the moving shadows in a stand of cottonwood trees, or marveled at how local river deposits could make the most wonderful adobe clay.

Shortly after the dessert course, Ben excused himself and walked to the front of the room, where an easel stood covered by a white sheet. While the space vibrated with anticipation, he explained that his new work portrayed a Lakota female ritual involving buffalo blood and a girl's passage to womanhood. Ben then invited me to remove the sheet from his painting.

"Wolfie, what . . . ?" Freddie was confused by the request.

I walked to the easel and lifted the sheet to reveal a four-foot square canvas. A neon crimson young girl with boyishly short hair stood in a pool of red, highlighted by a vivid white background. A keyhole overlaid by a green cottonwood leaf was prominently centered on her upper chest. Many Indian tribes considered a budding cottonwood leaf to be the sign of spring and the beginning of new life. The keyhole was symbolic of passing the threshold to maturity.

I read the painting's name to the audience. *"Red Water."* Then I continued with a paragraph Ben had written to explain the piece. "A holy man is speaking. 'We are buffalo on the plains and this is a waterhole; the water in it is red, for it is sacred and made by the Creator, and it is of and from Buffalo Women. Drink from it; be nourished; see that we are all connected, we are all related.' These words are from a buffalo ceremony where a girl becomes a woman." My voice quavered. I was overwhelmed at the enormity of the feelings that were welling up, along with visions of my own young ladies on their journey to womanhood. The scene in front of me blurred; I could see Freddie's outline but not her reaction. I stared above the heads, swallowed, and continued, *"Red Water* symbolizes nourishment and health, survival and protection through endurance. This is buffalo power, this is the 'red power.' "

There was barely enough oxygen left in

the room for me to gasp out the planned finale. "Ben has allowed me to buy this painting in honor of my young girls and my loving wife, who is devoted far beyond what is good for her health." Ben grabbed my shoulder, saving me any further explanation by leading the applause. I could no longer see Freddie's shape through the standing people, but then she appeared in front of me, her expression so complex and seductive that it could have inspired epic bravery or brought about world peace. Instead, it caused a coward to find faith. I managed to stay composed until Freddie put her arms around me and whispered, "Beyond touching, Wolfie."

10

June–September 2001 — Nebraska

If I had known that reception would be the highlight of my next few years, I would have been more careful to savor the look on Freddie's face and the warmth of my blessings that night. But it was over too quickly, and in another month, so was my Arizona exile. It was time to drive north.

When we arrived at the lake house for what was now being called my summer visit, I got out and walked to the back of the SUV to open the door for Comet, suddenly aware that the house seemed deserted. "Where are Cody and Sandoz?"

"All of the girls are busy, so the dogs are probably sleeping inside," Freddie said tensely. "Don't read anything into it. They are all growing up — things and people, seeing and doing . . ."

My stomach clenched as I said, "Come on, Comet. Let's go post bail for those four-legged inmates."

"Wolfie, before you go in, I have something to tell you," Freddie called after me, but I wasn't paying attention.

Even if I had been, it wouldn't have made a damn bit of difference. There had been moments in my life when bad news had seemed to stop time and paralyze every organ in my body. Fortunately, there were only a few such moments, like four years earlier when I had learned that my dad's heart valve had dissolved, along with his life, as he was lifting trout out of a Pagosa Springs river. Seeing Cody's emaciated back legs and prominent rib cage as he wriggled to greet me now joined the list. Only his wagging tail, dripping tongue, and joy-filled eyes kept me standing upright.

"When you're with him all the time, you just don't notice the signs as much," Freddie said softly. We were sitting at the kitchen table staring out the sliding glass doors, watching Comet and Sandoz romp up and down the beach. "I didn't even realize Cody was losing weight until your sister commented on it. The vet said that pain from hip dysplasia keeps him from using his back legs, causing his muscles to atrophy. Swimming is the best therapy. Good thing, since he spends all day in the water."

Cody had been the epitome of canine health when I had left last fall, his toned muscles on proud display as he shook water from his coat and strutted across the sand. The sight of his frail body was so jarring that I was still trying to process it as he came into the house, wiggling between me and Freddie. "That might explain his hips and the loss of mass in the hind area, but why is he so skinny?"

Wetness glinted in the corners of Freddie's eyes as she held out a treat for Cody's gulping acceptance. "The vet said he is about seven pounds lighter than last year, but he couldn't find any obvious causes — no heartworms or hookworms, and he still plays in the water all day long. He said that since Cody is thirteen, it might be the heat getting to him faster, making him less hungry when it's time to eat."

I had seen dogs look like Cody, and it was never the heat that was the problem. "I think that for a while he should sleep with me rather than Jackie," I said. "Maybe Cody's having trouble getting up at night and going down the steps to eat when he's hungry. I'll keep his food in my room." We had already decided that this summer I would sleep on the ground level so I wouldn't have to negotiate the stairs to the upper story. Cody bobbed his square head under my arm, telling me that great discoveries were waiting outside the sliding door and down the wooden steps. "He'll be okay." I'm not sure I spoke loudly enough for Freddie to hear.

Everyone called Cody my dog, and I spent more time with him than the rest of the family did, but he had adopted the girls when they were little. He had quickly assumed the role of activities director and lifeguard, never hesitating to snarl and show his teeth to scare the girls back to the house if they tried something dangerous, like playing too near the icy lake. Cody was Freddie's trusty pillow when she reclined in front of the hearth during the short, cold days of winter, the two of them seduced into napping by the glowing oak logs. He deserved a pain-free old age, and I was going to make sure he got every chance at it.

The following morning on her way out the door to work, Freddie handed me a list written on paper torn from one of Jackie's notebooks. "These are your doctor appointments for this month." Not only did Freddie work full-time and run the house, but I increasingly relied upon her to schedule doctor visits, keep track of my medications, and generally act as my personal assistant and nurse. I'm sure it would have been a relief if I had shown even the remotest interest in easing that burden, but my battles with pain were progressively robbing me of the ability to deal with any detail greater than just waking up and making it through the day. I rationalized my dependence on Freddie by reminding myself that every medical professional we knew felt compelled to seize control of all family issues involving health care. Freddie was no exception.

"If you have to cancel one of those appointments, be sure to call them," she instructed me.

"I'll be fine. And Comet needs the training; hospitals are totally new to her."

"That's good," Freddie said without much enthusiasm. The sparkling night in Sedona when I had presented her with Ben's painting felt as if it had taken place in our youth.

I hadn't seen Kylie or Lindsey since the previous September, nine months earlier. They were both staying in Omaha because of summer jobs and weren't sure when they could get out to the lake but would coordinate a visit. Jackie was beginning a softball schedule that had her playing in a different town every day. The afternoon I arrived, she greeted me with an awkward hug and then sprinted upstairs. When all three girls convened at the house several days later, their averted eyes told me that my presence made them uncomfortable. I couldn't blame them. I hadn't been involved in their lives for nearly two years now, and it had been four years since I was a fully operating member of the household — time during which the girls watched as I participated less as a father and withered away from their activities.

Although Kylie and Lindsey were both going to be in college and acting as if parents were as passé as rotary phones, there was still advice to give, finances to track, and late-night calls to answer. They were just getting their adult sea legs and naturally wanted support and love from their parents. Through my default, Freddie supplied 99 percent of that sustenance from our side of the family. Like a man adrift in a life raft, I could focus only on staying afloat.

At dinner that night, Freddie dutifully prompted the girls to tell me about their classes, boyfriends, and summer plans. They replied in the bright tones of people on a job interview, and I responded like an overeager houseguest. Finally the meal ended and Kylie and Lindsey drove back to the city.

At least I could be a doting parent to the

dogs. In light of the brutal midday temperatures, I insisted that Cody take an afternoon break in the air-conditioned house. I didn't reject the image of Cody's life ending while he was terrorizing the beachfront; I just didn't want it to be today or any other day. Besides, Sandoz was always in favor of a chilled nap. Whenever Cody stretched out on the floor next to my recliner, it was only moments before Sandoz plopped down against him. It was Comet who surprised me. Once the mass of golden hair was settled on the carpet, Comet would pick out an available space next to Cody and settle in. She'd snuggle her head on Cody's back, refusing to move until he was once again ready for the great outdoors.

Comet even allowed me to participate in an outside activity that did not include her. The only way I could enjoy the lake, other than standing in water up to my chin, was by motoring around on what the girls called the "handicapped Jet Ski." My personal flotation device was an eight-foot-long battery-powered pontoon boat with a plastic propeller mounted at the back of each float. A metal frame anchored a meshlike passenger sling between the pontoons. The propellers were controlled by metal switches on each armrest. Even in sticky, scorching weather, Cody and Sandoz would leap onto the boat, each taking a position at the head of a pontoon. The craft had a top speed of five miles per hour, not fast enough to generate even the tiniest wake. It looked like I was in a motorized lawn chair with two golden slippers on my feet. While baby Sandoz snoozed on one pontoon, Cody remained vigilant on the other, observing my movements and staying awake for as long as I could tolerate floating. He loved to go with me, and I loved having him. It gave us a chance to talk.

I was ensconced in the beach-level bedroom and sleeping alone. "I don't want to make your pain worse by moving around in bed" was Freddie's reason for staying in the master bedroom. Other than not knowing what was going on with the rest of the family, I had no quarrel with the arrangement. My books were placed on shelves lining both sides of the room's fireplace, and I had easy access to the beach from French doors opening to the outside patio. Comet didn't object because she had an unobstructed view of the whole stretch of sand from the door's windows. Plus, Cody was now her roommate. Comet still froze in strict disapproval, demanding exit, whenever I went outside. But once she saw me untie my "Jet

Ski," she leaped onto the bed, content with an uninterrupted nap. I had the feeling that Comet not only approved of my time with Cody, she encouraged it.

Comet became more businesslike over the summer as she learned to negotiate the medical facilities where Freddie had scheduled appointments with my longtime team of physicians. There was a big difference between those places and the retail stores in Sedona where I had trained Comet to tolerate groups of people. There the challenge was to get Comet to stay focused amid a bustling crowd, whereas in a hospital the whole environment was subdued. People waited in orderly lines, almost afraid to talk, as they watched medical personnel whispering to other patients. Couples sat with heads lowered and voices hushed. Piped music lulled other folks into an apparently comatose state.

From our very first visit to a medical office, Comet assumed a professional reserve that fit right in. Ignoring comments about her beauty and her service vest, she would march directly to the check-in counter, looking to neither the left nor the right. She adopted a bored attitude during the ensuing confusion about whether a dog should be allowed in examination rooms or near the arms of x-ray equipment and scanners. By this time, I had acquired business cards that summarized the ADA service animal dos and don'ts, highlighting Comet's right to access. The coat-and-tie demeanor exuded by this exotic animal demanded that a decision be made quickly, allowing us to efficiently complete our business. Inevitably, the technicians, nurses, and doctors would agree that Comet should be allowed to enter the sterile halls of the medical profession.

The hospital staff's strict attitude was actually a false front. After a Comet sighting, staff and doctors alike could be heard breaking out their baby patter. The sense of order often hid the genuine affection for animals that prevailed in every medical facility we visited. After the initial shock, an unspoken agreement would be reached: we won't question Comet as long as she remains professionally prim and proper. The treaty rules were suspended after a few visits to my regular providers. By then Comet had cast her spell, and instead of being treated like an unexpected IRS agent, she received the type of fawning attention normally reserved for celebrities. Receptionists may have needed to look at my records to remember my name, but Comet was hailed like an iconic athlete — Pelé, Nenê, Comet.

The series of doctor appointments validated Pam's assessment earlier in the year that I was getting worse. The medical report from the internist coordinating my care spelled it out: "Mr. Wolf has progressive paresthesia involving his legs and feet complicated by bilateral thigh and buttock pain along with dispersed lower back pains. There is no satisfactory medical or surgical remedy for his multilevel disc disease and at this time he is considered permanently and totally disabled."

I had known for a long time that I was on a road to nowhere with my junker of a body. But I had fantasized that it might be like Arizona state route 373, a stretch of road in the White Mountains known to locals as the highway to nowhere. On Route 373 you wind through seemingly endless mountain passes, with rarely another car in sight. Your passengers get restless and bored. They doubt your sense of direction or that there is any point in riding along with you. The medical version of the journey features rising uncertainty exacerbated by guilt and depression. Each road you think might lead out of the wilderness ends at the beginning. Herniated discs, dehydrated discs, spinal stenosis, deteriorating disc disease, scar tissue, neuropathy, bone spurs, arthritic facet joints; it doesn't matter all that much. The standard treatment is always the same: weight loss, ice, rest, aspirin, physical therapy, more drugs, and additional tests. Lost in a forest of frustration, you find yourself driving in circles, going nowhere.

But . . . at the terminus of Arizona's highway to nowhere is the resort community of Greer, a picturesque village nestled eighty-five hundred feet above sea level in a glorious mountain valley of fragrant pines. The Little Colorado River is birthed in the mountain range that rises above Greer, and it burbles through the middle of town in a twenty-foot-wide reflective ribbon filled with trout. Eating warm blueberry cobbler topped with a scoop of hard vanilla ice cream while reclining on the deck of the Rendezvous Diner is a definition of fine that not a lot of people ever know. Mix in a beauty so rare and quiet that it almost penetrates your skin, and a person can't help but feel that life is good — damn good — and the winding journey through the White Mountains was worth it. Who cares if in the winter it snows like it'll never stop and the temperature falls far below freezing? Experiencing a summer day like that makes bad weather just an annoyance.

That's what I had been trying to find these last few years — my own Greer and enough good days to make the bad ones not so bad. I had been lucky with that spinal fusion when I was sixteen. My surgeon had warned me at the time that it was not a total cure for what ailed me, but until the basketball game at the YMCA, the pain had been chased into the mountains often enough for me to frequently delight in life's homemade desserts. If my main hurdle was going to be back pain that was a few degrees more intense than bad, that wasn't an unacceptable price to pay.

Now, however, any illusions about what the future might hold for me evaporated. My pain specialist had called me in to review with him one of the quality-of-life charts that I periodically completed.

"Take a look at this," he said. "It wasn't too long ago that you were at level ten." I peeked at the paper. *Level 10: Go to work/ volunteer each day. Normal daily activities and social life. Active family life.* "Despite what we've been doing, you're now at a two or less." *Level 2: Get out of bed but not showered and dressed. Stay at home all day.*

"Steve, we need to change our approach. Some of my patients are having great results with the fentanyl transdermal system. I think you should try —"

"Wait a minute! Isn't that the stuff I heard about on the news? It's two hundred times more powerful than heroin! Didn't they say it used to be sold on the street as something called China White?" Comet stood as my voice got louder and she was now stretching in front of me, inviting my touch. I ignored her. I knew that the minute I started petting her, my indignation would lose some major velocity. But Comet's intrusion into the conversation had already had its effect. I lost my place in my planned pontification about God, flag, and the American way — just say no to drugs.

"Listen to me, Wolf." The doctor's sharp tone made me snap my mouth shut. "Pain is sometimes useful. It can force a patient to rest or to stop doing a harmful activity." But, he explained, untreated pain is like a muscle conditioned by lifting weights. The nerves become more effective at sending pain signals to the brain, so that eventually the brain will flinch even at harmless stimuli. The same input that was once tolerable hurts in increasingly damaging ways. Most medications cannot keep up with the escalating pain cycle without causing stomach ulcers or kidney damage. Strong narcotics can.

"We can get rid of most of the other medications that are causing you a lot of side effects," he concluded. My regimen of antidepressants, painkillers, and pills to quell the side effects of other pills had become so complicated that no one seemed to know where my medical problems stopped and the pharmaceutical ones began. I could see the doctor's point. "Quit being so paranoid about addiction," he reassured me. "Your body will come to need this medicine, but you won't turn into a drug vampire, constantly craving more and more."

And so I had agreed. It would take me a while to wean myself off the other medications and get used to the patch and the repulsive fentanyl "lollipops" that would stem any breakthrough pain, but I had plenty of time.

After the hectic first round of doctor appointments, I noticed that while I wasn't alone in my life, I was lonely. A few years back, another pain specialist had told me about a phenomenon he felt deserved some hard research. He had observed that a troubling emotional distance often develops between chronic pain sufferers and their friends and families. I didn't know it, but what I was beginning to perceive as tightly restrained anger and frustration in conversations that were directed at me was a common emotional response. People like me, who struggled for extended periods from conditions that couldn't be seen or given easily identifiable names, began to be cast in a different light over time.

What was beginning to plague my relationships with family and friends — a curse that would baffle me for the next several years — could be best summed up by a comment most patients with chronic back pain are subjected to sooner or later: "Shouldn't you be feeling better by now?" It's a stigma never voiced to amputees, or to those who are wheelchair-bound, or to patients diagnosed with cancer — those ailments are obvious or have a recognizable diagnostic label. What does pain look like? And if it's spinal pain, the tag assigned will most likely be medical mumbo jumbo not at all familiar to others. Degenerative disc disease. *So what? We all get older.* Postlaminectomy syndrome. *Huh?* Kyphoscoliosis and pseudoarthritis. *Oh, come on!* Ultimately, if there isn't any available medical cure: *Maybe it's all in your head.*

The sufferer is then faced with an isolating conundrum. If I talk about my misery, I risk being viewed as a hypochondriac, a

Debbie Downer who wreaks havoc on any normal social setting. On the other hand, if I hide my pain, I'm viewed either as a hopeless stoic who refuses help or someone who would *have* to be complaining if he were in that much pain. Current research not only validates these types of anecdotal observations, it also shows that this stigmatization actually magnifies the patient's physical suffering. That shouldn't be a big surprise. Depression and pain often use the same nerve pathways.

At the time, though, all I was aware of was antipathy, somewhat vague but unmistakable nonetheless, which was focused at me. Family and friends were progressively absent from my life. Associates stopped returning my phone calls. Daughters didn't come home for the weekend. Freddie started working later. Friends were always golfing or out of town. Nobody said it to my face, but I knew what they were thinking: *You're addicted to medication . . . You've let your body go to hell . . . You need to see some better doctors . . . You haven't explored new treatments . . . You're doing things that make it worse . . . You're just not trying hard enough.* Was I really that much of a miserable son of a bitch? Or was my distrust valid? It was easy to be paranoid when the only other thing I could think about was that I hurt like hell. Only Comet, Cody, and Sandoz seemed to enjoy my company.

Those poor dogs! They became my full-time companions and psychologists. My health complaints were directed at three creatures who would much rather have been racing down the beach. They patiently listened, occasionally raising their eyebrows or cocking their heads as I muttered a nonstop inventory of past mistakes. Comet attended every one of my doctor consultations and ego-sucking tests. My handicapped Jet Ski was a river casino of wild thoughts about the future, captained by loyal Cody, who was now crawling to the dock almost as slowly as I was.

It's a shame that it had to be Cody who roused me from my self-absorption. At about 3:00 a.m. one morning I was awakened by a raspy, coughing choke coming from the floor. It had started a couple of weeks earlier with an occasional cough followed by a retching noise that made me think a fish bone was stuck in Cody's throat. I couldn't feel any foreign objects when I thrust my finger down the length of his tongue, nor could I detect any lumps from a physical exam of his throat. The vet wasn't excited about subjecting a thirteen-year-old dog to x-rays. I bought a plastic syringe and began squirting cough medicine into his mouth before bedtime. Tonight, though, the sound had changed from retching to the wheeze of labored breathing.

"It's okay, buddy." Cody was trying to get to his paws, but I gently lowered him to his bed. "What's the matter?" The question was part of my rubbing investigation of his neck. I didn't expect the answer I got: a round mass beneath the fur just below his throat.

Cody was the gentlest, most obedient dog I have ever had the pleasure of knowing. He insisted on walking into the vet's office that dawn, but he could no longer leap onto the exam table. He allowed me to help the vet lift him onto the stainless table without protest. He always trusted me. But on this occasion, Cody's black eyes staring from beneath prominent raised eyebrows pleaded with me to take him out of there. The streaks down my cheeks told him I just couldn't do that right now. I should have. A lump was clogging Cody's airway, making it hard for him to swallow anything. It was as if the thyroid tumor diagnosis was what my longtime friend was trying to avoid. As long as Cody didn't know how sick he was, he could go on forever. Once voice was given to the problem, it was as if the knowledge killed him. Cody was gone within the week.

A few days after his passing, despite intense pain shooting down my legs into my toes, I floated on the lake long into the afternoon. I knew the pontoon boat's batteries were nearly as exhausted as I was, but I still couldn't perform this final task. It felt like it wasn't just an end; it was the end. After a day spent blistering my nose and shoulders, I couldn't find any answers, other than that I was lost. Saying good-bye shouldn't have been on my summer itinerary. I dared anybody to tell me that life was fair — or worse, that this was just part of living. I couldn't have hated being alive more. I dumped Cody's ashes into the lake.

All summer long, the normal colors of home seemed diminished, as if I were viewing them through a dingy filter. I was continually stalked by an old guy with a beard asking if he could harvest my oats with his scythe. Instead, he found Cody. I couldn't get out of Nebraska fast enough.

11

Freddie smiled briefly and waved from the window of the airport shuttle, and as it pulled away I lifted my hand in a salute. This time there had been no tears or urgent pleas for me to take better care of myself. "And that's a good thing," I said aloud as Comet and I turned and walked back inside the Sedona house. But a nagging worry lay just beneath the surface. The damping down of Freddie's emotions had me concerned, especially because once she admitted what was causing it, I might become a permanent resident of Arizona. We were farther apart than ever, yet I didn't know what I could do about it.

Unlike me, Comet was blooming with health and eager to explore the savory Sedona autumn. Emily was growing up and less likely to be around to walk Comet on a moment's notice, so Comet worked out her

208

own solution. After one early afternoon nap I grudgingly peeled the sheets away, intending to let her out back for her break. She refused to exit. "Fine. Don't go to the bathroom. I don't care." I left her by the slider and closed my bedroom door. Comet opened it. I slammed it shut. Comet opened it. I glared at her shameless expression. *"What?"* I demanded.

I settled on the end of the bed and peevishly watched Comet trot out of the room. I was just about to slam the door again when she returned, lowering her chest and thumping the floor with her front paws in a drum roll, repeating the sequence several more times with a couple of spinning twists thrown in for dramatic effect. I rolled my eyes in frustration, recalling Mark Twain's astute observation: "Comet, I want you to know that few things are harder to put up with than the annoyance of a good example."

I felt like Victor Frankenstein. Comet was my monster. She now had a job to do, and she was going to do it — period, exclamation mark. Her duty didn't end at getting me out of bed; it included getting me out of the house. She was through with allowing me to skimp on her daily walks. Within a few days, I found that the time outside cleared my head. After a week, I had mentally assembled a to-do list for Comet and me to tackle together. The first item on the list was something I knew would take a burden off Freddie: I wanted to be able to travel without her help. Now that I was using a fentanyl patch, I had to get recertified at my Omaha doctor's office every few months, but the drive was too grueling for me to tackle alone. I was going to have to fly back and forth either by myself or with Comet. Luckily, most of my trips began and ended in Phoenix, where my mother lived, or in Omaha, where I had family to pick me up. I could always check my bags at the curb. That left just one hurdle: getting from the curb to the gate on time. Although every airport has porters who can push a wheelchair or provide a cart for transportation, at busy hubs like Phoenix the odds of getting that help when you need it are remote. A better way would be to have a personal assistant pull me through the terminal.

Pulling something, especially if it's heavy and hard to get moving, is not a natural activity for dogs. Huskies are trained to pull sleds, but would Comet be strong enough to pull a wheelchair with a full-grown man in it? I had no doubt that she would. Not only are greys strong, they also have a high pain threshold and know how to use their energy efficiently. A greyhound probably couldn't pull a heavily loaded sled through the snow like a husky, but I wasn't asking for that. I didn't even need to start with a wheelchair.

"Comet, you have no idea how much I hate trying to grocery shop while pushing that damn cart," I told her. My little pride demon kept me from using the motorized carts at the store. A shopping cart could be an ideal vehicle for Comet to practice on before we braved a wheelchair in an airport. My first step would be to get her accustomed to being in the grocery store while I pushed the cart. Weber's IGA would be a good place to practice. It wasn't a large supermarket, and the staff knew every regular shopper by name. The family owners had allowed Maggie to conduct greyhound fund-raising on site for several years, and they had come to adore the breed as much as I did.

On our first visit to the IGA, I walked inside with Comet as if we shopped together all the time. Looping one end of her leash over my left wrist while I leaned on the cane in my right hand, I slowly nudged a shopping cart down an aisle. The assistant manager, who examined Comet's service vest and the card explaining the ADA, spied on our circus act from the fresh vegetable section, then lurked behind us and monitored our progress from aisle to aisle. Dogs were prohibited from entering the store for good reason, and he wasn't about to be fooled by this service stuff, even if I was somebody he knew. After all, who wanted dog hair in their celery?

Comet and I inched our way down the aisle, Comet tracing my steps from the shelves back to the cart. Then I would try to balance on my cane as I pushed the cart with one hand, often leaning on Comet for support. It was a ponderous, time-consuming process but surprisingly enjoyable. I found myself watching Comet like a proud daddy as her nose twitched, absorbing yeasty fresh-baked-bread smells mingling with metallic, primal blood odors from butchered slabs of steak. Although her eyes hungrily scanned the slick packages of meat and poultry, she refrained from ripping open the prizes inside. *Good girl!* By the time we reached the frozen food section that ran down the center of the store, we were a well-coordinated vision of competence. I was a rooster at dawn as we strolled along, silently crowing about Comet's working attitude. She didn't even startle when I dropped grocery items.

At the far end of each aisle I could see Inspector Clouseau of the IGA peeking around the corner, probably anticipating Comet attacking the nearest shopper like a starving hyena. He was rewarded only because my path to the checkout lane took us through an assortment of dog food and pet supplies. I didn't see Comet's head move at all, but there was no mistaking the squeaking noise as she crunched on a rubber bone.

"Comet! Give me that!"

"You're going to have to buy that toy. There's no way we could sell it now!" An *I knew it!* expression radiated from Clouseau's red face.

"Is Comet's breath so bad that it scarred that bone for life?" The employee squirmed and looked at me uncertainly. "I'll have you know that she has stolen toys from better places than this without anybody protesting. She is, after all, Comet," I proclaimed.

"Well, I suppose we could put the bone back on the shelf." He reached out and tried to swipe the toy from Comet's mouth. Comet clenched down on it and ignored him, fixing her glare on a shelf over his shoulder as if to indicate that she did not understand his peasant language. I decided some mercy was in order.

"Oh, I guess we'll just have to buy the darn thing," I said, laughing. "Come on, Comet, let's go check out."

Before our next in-store session, I made sure Comet's kleptomania was extinguished. Figuring that her attraction to a squeaky toy would be far less intense than her slobbering desire to nab a liver treat, I placed said treat at nose level on the kitchen table. It took me less than an hour to teach Comet that when she was wearing her service vest she was not entitled to grab a treat or anything else. During our training excursions, I had noticed a subtle change in Comet's posture whenever someone exclaimed, "You look so pretty in your purple vest." Her head would rise a few inches and her ears would almost imperceptibly perk, a canine version of a puffed chest. Comet had gradually connected her finery to her right to adopt a standoffish attitude around strangers — *You can look, but don't touch.* That was precisely the type of demeanor that I wanted when she was wearing her working clothes. On those occasions, she should focus on me unless I gave her express permission to do otherwise, and that included resisting toys at the grocery store.

After several successful training forays into

the IGA, I felt comfortable enough to proceed to the next step. Freddie was coming to Sedona for a brief visit, so she could team-teach with me. This time I would pick her up at Phoenix's Sky Harbor airport. I was hoping that in Phoenix I could find a crucial item that none of Sedona's pet supply stores seemed to carry, a working harness for Comet. None of the harnesses I had found were designed for an abnormally large chest that tapered sharply to a dainty stomach more suited to a toy poodle. I had seen boxers wearing harnesses, and their anatomy was not entirely different; it was just smaller. My best chance of finding something like that was at a large chain pet supply store, one of which was on the way to the airport.

"What do you think, Comet?" She and I stood just inside the store entrance. My question was rhetorical — Comet's ears were pointing straight at the ceiling, her eyes were stretched wide, and her nose twitched at the mysterious scents flying through the air. Her body was frozen in place, shivering with delight at the sights and smells. *If ever there was a kid in a candy store . . .* She was so entranced that she didn't even notice the other dogs and owners wandering through the store. I decided that a tour was in order, giving Comet's mind a chance to catch up to her vibrating senses while she examined hamsters and snakes, fish and reptiles, and every type of pet food known to mankind.

As we approached the back of the store, a painfully high-pitched shriek blared from a far corner. Comet stopped in her tracks. Her body began to palpitate so rapidly I thought her heart was fibrillating. Suddenly she yanked on the leash and started dragging me toward the sound. Seconds later we were standing in front of a parrot cage, where the orange and green bird strutted back and forth squawking and screeching. Ears perked and eyes like lasers, Comet hunkered down into a stalking-cat position, ready to pounce. "No!" I shouted, tugging her away. "I can't afford a thousand-dollar bag of feathers." From that day forward, any time we entered a large pet store, Comet prowled around looking for that annoying parrot.

We had better luck in the leash and harness aisle. After wrestling Comet into a number of harnesses, I settled on a black and saddle-toned rig with gold fittings. Comet approved. The look was striking against her cinnamon and black striped coat, and I think she knew it. She didn't object one bit when I left the harness on her for our drive to pick up Freddie.

As we approached the airport, it occurred to me that Comet might have a complete sensory overload if I took her into the terminal. But the greyhound's enthusiasm with her new harness was infectious. "I guess you'll have to get used to the airport sometime," I said, attaching her leash. Comet jumped from the back hatch with the alacrity of a panther.

We took the elevator from the parking garage and exited on the third floor. As we rounded a corner, the retail midway of Sky Harbor unfolded in a splash of neon signs and an undulating rainbow of cultures and clothing. The air was humming with cell phone conversations, laughter, a loud-speaker announcing arrivals and departures, and the eager voices of hundreds of travelers. Comet's jaw all but dropped.

I vividly recall my first time at the circus: flashing lights, air-whistling calliope sounds, smells of cotton candy and peanut shells, lions and elephants, freaks of the midway, and sequined aerialists swinging through the smoky heights of the big top. It was a sensory banquet so rich that I was dizzy, almost ill, even before my cousin handed me my first cigarette. I'm sure I looked as dumbstruck as I felt.

The same openmouthed, eye-bulging expression was on Comet's face as we took in the sights and sounds of Concourse A. She repeatedly stopped in the middle of traffic, her eyes roaming in a 180-degree panorama, digesting everything in sight before turning her body in the other direction to complete the dazed inventory. It was one of the few times in our relationship that Comet had no idea if I was anywhere in the vicinity. When we spotted Freddie at her arrival gate, Comet pranced at the end of the lead as if she couldn't wait to tell her about the astounding experience that lay in store for us on our journey back through the crowds.

"Comet, you look so elegantly professional in your new outfit," Freddie gushed. We giggled like a junior high couple on a first date as we followed Comet back through the terminal. Now she sped along as if she owned the place, tugging us this way and that to show us the scent of cinnamon rolls or grilling burgers. We were barely at one location before Comet zoomed off toward something else.

After we climbed into the SUV and Freddie settled into the driver's seat, she grinned at me. "I was going to tell you how pale you look, but I'd rather talk about that

218

big smile stuck on your mug. I didn't realize that you missed me so much."

"I can't even tell you how much fun that
was!" I chortled, quickly adding, "But I'm
smiling because you're here."

"That's okay, Wolfie." There was a quiet
pause as our eyes briefly locked. "I almost
forgot what a happy Wolf looked like." She
glanced at Comet in the rearview mirror.
"We might have to get Comet a different
outfit. That purple vest under the harness
won't be up to her standards."

The drive back to Sedona gave me time
to explain my thoughts about flying home
with Comet as my assistant. "My plan is to
train her to pull a grocery cart first, then a
wheelchair." Freddie's eyes narrowed in an
amused squint as she continued driving.
"You got here just in time to help." Her
eyebrows shot up and her mouth pursed in
an "uh-oh" shape, but at least she didn't
say no.

I gave Freddie a full day to unwind before
hustling her over to the IGA. Because
Comet was now an accepted customer,
Inspector Clouseau no longer tailed us. I
filled a shopping cart with a few heavy
items, looped Comet's leash through the
front frame of the cart, and handed the
leash to Freddie. "Snap that onto Comet's

harness," I directed her. "The cart has some load, but I don't think it's too much to start out with. I'll handle the cart from behind so it doesn't run into Comet's heels when she stops. Plus she'll get used to me being back here while she's working."

"Am I supposed to give her a treat to get her moving or just as a reward for pulling?" Freddie whispered the question and hunkered in front of the cart, obviously trying to hide.

I had no idea how to teach a dog to pull, so it would have to be trial and error. "If you walk in front, Comet will try to walk with you. Just don't let her panic when she feels the leash tighten. We'll start by giving her a treat if she doesn't spook when she feels the weight." I took a sheepish peek down the aisle to see if we were attracting attention.

"Come here, Comet — here, girl." Freddie backed down the aisle several paces, facing Comet while maintaining her stealth posture. Comet watched Freddie's progress for a brief moment and then turned her head, glaring a demand that I call a halt to this humiliating public display. "Come here, sweetie," coaxed Freddie. Comet refused to move. "I thought you said she would walk with me."

Several people passed by with loaded carts and quizzical looks. I suspected that the grocery patrol would not be far behind. "Let's try something else. Why don't I walk in front while you drive the cart?" *Come on, Comet — we have to get moving if we don't want to get kicked out of here!* I exchanged places with Freddie, scratched Comet's ears, and caned farther down the aisle. Comet immediately followed, only to come to an abrupt stop when she felt the weight pull at her harness. Comet turned to admonish Freddie, clearly communicating that practical jokes were not appreciated at work. "Come on, girl, I need the cart." I laughed softly, encouraging Comet with an outstretched hand and a liver snap. "Come on!" I was starting to sound desperate.

Comet strained, then stopped, once again taking a backward glance. Freddie pushed the cart forward, relieving the tension on Comet's harness. Comet turned back to me, taking another step and tugging as Freddie pushed. After two more steps Comet pulled the treat from my hand. We slowly made our way past assorted groceries, the cart jumping and jerking each time Comet popped the clutch. Tasty treats and my joy at her willingness to keep going increased Comet's confidence.

By the time we passed the bread and made our way across the store to the drinks, the cart followed Comet like a beer wagon behind Clydesdales. I added a twelve-pack of Oak Creek lager to complete the effect. Employees stopped stocking shelves when we passed by, greeting us with wide eyes and smiles of disbelief. I returned their looks with a posture of worldly condescension. *These people act like they've never seen a greyhound pulling a grocery cart before!*

Over the next couple of days we bought a whole lot of groceries and fine-tuned our cart-pulling routine. On one occasion, after Comet's lurch toward the treat in Freddie's hand caused me to lose my grip on the cart and crash to the floor, I decided that Comet should not pull until I gave the command with a click of my tongue. Comet herself figured out that standing too close to the glass door in the frozen goods section was another hazard. If I lost my balance, the door had a tendency to fly open and smack any nose within its radius. Comet developed her own version of respectful distance, seeking refuge by the cart whenever we came to a stop. *Good thinking, Comet!*

We also developed a game plan for restricted traffic flow, especially in areas crowded by stacks of breakable items. On our final trip through IGA before Freddie's departure, we left Comet parked between cardboard display columns while we decided on a bottle of wine to accompany Freddie's planned rack of lamb. Comet wasn't quite sure of the protocol for times when I wandered away from our groceries, and as she edged closer to us, several stacked cases of expensive wine began to wobble. One toppled over, but it fell directly onto our groceries, saving us from permanent exile. *Good catch, Comet.*

In the days that followed, Comet and I worked out the kinks. It wasn't long before she would stand and stay wherever she was left with the cart. She knew not to move forward without my command and to halt slowly when I said stop, so as not to get hit from behind. Comet's dedication to her shopping cart training was difficult to put into perspective. Was this behavior as unusual as I thought it was?

Members of the greyhound community with whom I periodically talked expressed dead certainty that their greyhounds would never even consider pulling a load of any type. Most of these people thought I was exaggerating until several of them had the opportunity to see Comet at work. Their amazement matched mine. I think that their laugh-aloud astonishment was due to the fact that Comet's work wasn't some kind of trick. She wasn't balancing on her hind legs while wearing a frilly dress and dancing to the rhythms of the merengue. She was assisting me with tasks that were becoming impossible to do alone — opening doors, helping me lift myself from chairs and climb up and down stairs, and now pulling my grocery cart.

When she wasn't working, Comet continued her duties of therapist, encouraging me to get up, to walk, to get out of the house, and to meet wonderful people. She was no longer just a greyhound; she was a working dog, a service dog. Maybe not yet perfect but clearly able and willing to get there. Every night, as darkness settled and the heavens sparked alive, I found myself marveling at the long-tailed Comet that circled around my chair, even as she slumbered nearby. *Thank you, Comet.*

12

With the grocery cart training under our belts, it was time for Comet's ultimate challenge: pulling me in a wheelchair through Sky Harbor airport. Considering her initial reaction to the concourse, I was bracing myself for an interesting time. The drive to Phoenix was a challenge all its own. The only way to get there from Sedona was via I-17, a steep, narrow highway that descended nearly three thousand feet in about eighty miles. I'm not an overly religious man, but before we began the winding mountain pass, I would pull over to the shoulder, get out of the SUV with Comet, and murmur a brief prayer. I could scarcely count the number of accidents we had witnessed on this road. Making matters worse, I-17 was the only major north-south route in the whole state of Arizona, so every southbound tractor-trailer rig was forced to squeeze down it.

Our first two return trips to the airport were practice runs where Comet and I simply walked around the concourse together. During these visits, Comet gleefully absorbed new information, a rapt student intrigued by the controlled chaos all around her. Before long she was making her way through the terminal as casually and anonymously as an employee, except for the times when she would freeze in midstride, ears perked and eyes pinned on some new discovery, all but shouting, *Look at that!*

On our third visit the real work began. I borrowed one of the airport wheelchairs and pushed it to the main concourse, where Comet proceeded to sniff it from bow to stern. Merely getting the thing to the concourse had left me aching and sweaty. I needed to sit down. Ignoring annoyed glances from uniformed aides pushing other wheelchairs toward the gates, I attached the lead to Comet's harness and collapsed into the seat. One advantage of our grocery store training was that Comet knew how to respond to my commands of "Let's go," "Left," or "Right." When I looped the leash around my wrist and said, "Let's go," she was confused only briefly. She moved forward slowly, slightly jerking at my weight, and then she settled into a comfortable trot, correctly assuming that she was to walk in the same direction as the main traffic flow. I held the leash straight out in front of me, coasting along behind Comet as jauntily as the captain of a new skiff. *Hey, this is easy!*

That carefree feeling lasted about thirty seconds, until we sailed past a souvenir shop. Almost in slow motion, a woman floated into my peripheral vision, exiting the shop with luggage in tow and coffee in hand. "Stop! Left!" I yelled, but Comet had already slammed to a halt as the lady stumbled on tiptoes around her. It never dawned on me that I couldn't properly control the wheelchair's brake levers with only one hand. That became clear as the chair rammed Comet's heels and she leaped forward into the startled lady's legs, causing a domino effect of splattered coffee and sputtered expletives.

"I'm so sorry! We're in training —"

"Piss off!" the woman spat in a British accent before stomping away. A security guard materialized. Comet nuzzled up next to him with a hopeful look on her face — *Oh my! A man in uniform!* — and her flirtatiousness worked in our favor. The guard suggested we continue our training in a less-populated part of the airport, but he assured us, "That

227

sweet dog is welcome back here anytime."

Comet watched as he disappeared into the crowd. "You can put your tongue back in your mouth, Comet. He's gone." I pondered my next move while people swirled around us. "I might have to get a body clip to make this a little easier. Plus, if I'm hooked directly to you it'll be harder for you to drag me into a corner and leave me there while you go looking for Officer Dreamboat." All big eyes and innocence, Comet acted as if the thought had never entered her head.

But where would I find a body clip? I realized I was wearing one already, around my waist. "Okay, Comet. I'm going to wrap my belt around my chest so that if you pull hard, it won't hurt me too much." I put my jacket on over my makeshift harness to minimize any further humiliation for Comet. She watched me attach her leash to the belt buckle, her head tilted in a question mark. But it only took one pull for her to figure out that I wouldn't be ejected from the chair even though I was not gripping the leash in my hand.

In short order we were cruising the concourses at a fairly rapid clip. We flew past passengers watching from moving walkways, their delighted faces a blur as I tried to control this forty-five-mile-per-hour missile.

"Slow down, Comet!" Between warnings, I helped Comet navigate turns by partially braking only one wheel, and I cleared our path by yelling, "Beep, beep!" to scatter any groups of people who stood in our way. Now that Comet knew the chair would not bump her from behind, she cornered and braked like a Lamborghini. It was so much fun that not even Her Highness had time to be self-conscious.

The only real problems we encountered were Comet's sudden one-wheeled, ninety-degree turns toward crying babies. She uncannily detected the faintest cries while sailing through the white noise. As far as I knew, Comet had never been around a baby before. On our other outings I had noticed perked ears and a pulled leash in the direction of baby sounds, but I had always guided her away. Roaming without such close control, Comet seemed compelled to identify the cause of the high-pitched wails.

The first time it happened I was taken by surprise, barely able to stay seated while forcing the airborne wheel back to ground in a tile-screeching slam. Riding sheep at a junior rodeo was safer. When we arrived at the source, Comet pulled so hard forward on the braked chair and my harness that she nearly broke my desperate grip on the armrests. I begged apologies through the throbbing pain, hoping I could prevent a maternal meltdown, only to be baffled when the smiling mother asked if her baby could touch Comet's fur. Still, for safety reasons (my own), I decided that Comet would only be allowed to seek out crying babies if I gave my permission. After a couple of braked stops that yanked her backward like a roped steer, Comet agreed to the new limitations.

All in all, I'd be lying if I said that training Comet to pull my wheelchair was difficult. Even when she was simply standing still in the concourse, Comet absorbed knowledge from the pulsing pool of human interaction. By our fifth airport training session, she was shuttling me through Sky Harbor like a rickshaw driver through the streets of old Saigon.

Working so intensely with Comet made me wonder all over again at the seemingly contrary traits that coexisted within this dog. She grasped my needs quickly, almost intuitively, and readily accepted my instruction. She acknowledged my alpha role in our relationship and clearly took pride in helping me. Yet she was also stubbornly independent and didn't hesitate to let me know when I was asking her to do something she deemed beneath her station. For instance, when I tried to train her to shake hands, she found the task overwhelmingly stupid and simply sat and ignored me. And unless we were at the lake, my tossed tennis balls were met with an expression that seemed to say, *You poor, deluded man. I would no sooner fetch a ball from dry land than I would hunt quail for dinner. What would be the point?*

My friends in the rescue groups often recited a familiar list of the greyhound breed's attributes: "Quizzical, shy, sensitive, gentle, superior intelligence, surprising independence, athletic, quiet, and lovingly loyal." But these words fell short of describing the experience of living with Comet. Something else had to help explain why, throughout history, greyhounds had occupied a unique spot in the hearts and imaginations of human beings. Homer wrote that the only creature to recognize Odysseus upon his return was his greyhound Argos, who then "passed into the darkness of death, now that he had seen his master once more after twenty years." Frederick the Great was buried with his greyhound pack. In eleventh-century England, a person could be tried for murder if he killed a grey, even accidentally. Greyhounds traveled with explorers, accompanied generals, and adorned the suites of royalty.

Research and personal observation led me to conclude that greyhounds were unusual because of the way the breed evolved. Greys are generally acknowledged to be one of the original canine breeds from which all domestic dogs descended. Today's greyhound is one short evolutionary step removed from its Asian wolf ancestors, who were first domesticated about forty thousand years ago. Greyhounds must not be far behind on the domestication time line. One of the earliest depictions of a greyhoundlike animal is a carving in an Egyptian crypt from 2751 BCE that shows a pack of greys bringing down a deer. The carving illustrates two primary greyhound characteristics, teamwork and intelligence, that have been valued by humans for millennia. Over the ages these originally primal traits have been encouraged through breeding, and it is the teamwork aspect that might account for the greyhound's unique mix of independence, cleverness, and cooperation.

For thousands of years prior to being tamed, greyhounds lived in packs that required them to pool their respective skills. While they have always been known primarily for their speed and sight, greys were also blessed with exceptional senses of hearing and smell. As with any group, abilities varied from one member to the next, and they learned while in the wild to employ each individual's skill to the pack's advantage. When hunting, a greyhound pack learned to use this coordination on the fly, spontaneously adjusting pursuit strategies in the middle of a chase. The need to adjust during a hunt promoted individual resourcefulness as well as collaboration, which may partly account for the breed's strong independent streak today.

At the same time, aggression was subdued in the wild for the benefit of the group. It wasn't an efficient hunt if you were fighting with one another. Prior to domesticated coursing, greyhounds grew as a peaceful family, using their speed, sight, and intelligence rather than ferocity in order to catch their food. Since becoming domesticated, the breed has enjoyed a long history of working with humans to chase and capture both large and small game for eating, everything from deer to rabbits. Of course, their eventual rank as royal animals altered their status from hunters to coursing athletes, but the attributes of intelligent cooperation and lack of aggression originated in those ancient genes.

Today's rescued racers also grow up in a

pack, a large birth litter that is slowly culled into the groups of dogs that are housed together at the track, where they are then separately caged. From that point on, unless the dog is a winner or a breeder, it is isolated from both the wild and the normal outside world. The retired grey's socialization problems arise from lack of worldly exposure, not from an innate fear of or hostility toward humans. Since it is humans who assume the alpha role among the group of kenneled dogs, rescued greyhounds accept people in leadership roles more readily than do many other breeds. This, coupled with their lack of aggression, makes them one of the gentlest breeds in existence.

Greyhounds are designed to conserve energy until it is absolutely needed. This is one reason they don't often bark, and it's also why one or two tail wags is more than enough of a greeting. These dogs observe the world from a quiet place. I'm convinced that this slower, calmer pace is the main reason greyhounds are so sharply attuned to events going on around them and to their human companions. That would explain why they are able to learn so quickly and intuitively, as Comet seemed to do with me.

While Comet exhibited most of the traits one would expect of a retired racer, there was something unusual about her demeanor. She seemed to exude a dignified wisdom that whispered, *I understand*. When she laid her head on my chest during a particularly bad day, it wasn't out of distress. When she watched over me for unbearably long periods of time between bathroom breaks, it wasn't because she felt sorry for me. Comet *really did know* what I was going through. And she accepted that there might not be anything she could do about it. Her actions weren't sympathy. They were empathy — compassion, responsiveness, and identification, all served up with only the slightest pinch of pity.

I never had the feeling that Comet was a person in a dog's body or that she wanted to be human. She was quite comfortable in her own skin, satisfied with being a greyhound. Comet and I were not the same species, but we were equals on this journey together, and we shared a mutual respect that went far deeper than the word *rescue* could convey.

I planned to fly with Comet to Omaha in early November without help from Freddie. Unfortunately, the process of adjusting to new medication while withdrawing from some of the antidepressant, antineuropathy drugs was beating the living daylights out of me. I had the energy of a rag doll. After a few phone conversations with me that must have been only semicoherent, my wife arrived to help Comet and me navigate our first airplane trip.

Comet was used to Sky Harbor by now and didn't register that anything different from our usual tour of the concourse was about to take place. After we assured the ticketing agents and security staff that she was a service animal and her presence on the plane was protected by the ADA, Freddie, Comet, and I made our way to the gate.

"I can't believe how professional she is," Freddie said as she held a cup of water for Comet. "She stands right beside you like a personal nurse. I sure hope she still thinks she's Florence Nightingale inside the plane." A loudspeaker announced, "People needing assistance may now board," and the three of us moved to the front of the line.

Comet didn't display anxiousness the same way other dogs did. Still, I had learned the slight tells in her confident facade. Going down the gangway to the plane's entrance, she glanced frequently to the left and right at the walls that prevented escape and then looked back at me to make sure I hadn't abandoned ship. She stopped short and froze when the flight attendant greeted our arrival with a "Well, aren't you pretty?" A generous ticketing agent had upgraded our seats, and the attendant continued, "Of course you're first class." The woman's soothing tone reassured Comet, and I could almost feel Comet growing taller as she entered the plane.

"This dog's a damn babe magnet," Freddie remarked as she threw the carry-on into the luggage bin. I'll admit that I didn't discourage any of the fawning attention Comet attracted in the first-class cabin. I enthusiastically talked about the virtues of the breed and eagerly responded to the unanimous observation of all three attendants that "greyhounds aren't usually helper dogs." Comet stood at attention in the space in front of my bulkhead seat, basking in the affectionate crooning. Meanwhile, Freddie spurned the flight attendant's repeated offers (to me) of a morning cordial. "He'll have some coffee and a glass of orange juice without vodka," she instructed. As the attendant moved down the aisle, Freddie said, "We're going to have to rethink this idea of you flying by yourself. Look at what's happening even when I'm here!"

Comet's ears jolted straight up as the plane taxied for takeoff. She accommodated the swaying by subtly engaging her four-paw-drive system. "It's okay, girl," I said, scratching her upturned ears and the bottom of her chin. Just when I felt Comet's body relax, the plane's throttles kicked in, causing her to slam backward into my knees. Her startled dog eyes blinked up at me — *What the heck was that?* We were halfway to Omaha before Comet finally flopped onto the blanket we had brought for her.

Comet and I traveled back and forth to Nebraska by ourselves twice that fall to get recertified for the fentanyl patch. I couldn't really tell how well the drug was working. So many places in my spine, legs, and feet were burning and cramping that it was no longer possible to figure out what was causing the pain, and I had started getting anxiety attacks whenever I was hit with unpleasant news. Amid this alarming decline, the highlight of my autumn became the plane rides with Comet. Curbside luggage service, along with expedited ticketing and security checks owing to my disabled status, made it easy to bring her along. All I needed was a carry-on with a blanket, a bottle of water, and a dish.

When our plane landed in Omaha or Phoenix, the flight attendants would open the door to a waiting wheelchair. After one of them pushed me up the walkway, I would decline further help, allowing Comet to take over so that I could revel in racing through the terminal. As we sped along, colorful concessionaire blocks mingled with glimpses of arms, legs, and open mouths in a cubist diorama that could have been stolen from Picasso. The flying scenery left me as giddy as a teenager on his first joyride.

My body might be failing me, but I still had the capacity to marvel at the sight of Comet pulling that chair. She reminded me of the magnificent Sandhill cranes that migrated through Nebraska, their long necks stretching into the wind and their skinny legs extending out behind them. Instead of a six-foot pair of wings, Comet's hind muscles propelled us swiftly forward. Her movements seemed as ancient as the cranes'. I couldn't help but think of all the men, from Odysseus onward, who had thrilled at their greyhounds' effortless power.

My third trip alone with Comet took us back to Omaha for Christmas. I was some-what at peace because all three girls seemed to have arranged their lives in a tidy, responsible order. Jackie was enjoying her junior year at Fremont High. Kylie had received two full scholarship offers from her law schools of choice. Lindsey was on an academic scholarship in the marine biology program at the University of Tampa. Maybe now that they were a little older, they would feel more comfortable around me and we could have a few spirited arguments about life and politics, the way we used to.

But it's never that simple. Kylie and Lindsey stuck around for only one day after I arrived and then left on a holiday trip to Florida with their mother. Jackie vanished to a YMCA horse camp to be a counselor. One evening after the girls had departed, Freddie prepared a dinner for two and tried her mightiest to make it romantic. Candlelight shimmered on the ceiling, and a bottle of French Bordeaux warmed our weary bodies. Then Freddie let slip that one of the girls had dared to reconsider her plans. In seconds I was on high alert.

"What do you mean Lindsey's not happy? When did this come about?" I was talking louder than I should have, but I was upset.

"Lindsey wanted to work directly with marine life. Those jobs are almost non-existent for new graduates. She was willing to work her way up, but then she found out that her ears won't pressurize when she scuba dives. Plus she's afraid of the ocean. It all goes back to that girl having her leg cut off." Two years before Lindsey graduated high school, a young woman we knew had tumbled out of a motorboat on the Missouri River. Her entire leg was severed by the boat's propeller, and the event had an enormous impact on Lindsey. Still, that hadn't prevented her from pursuing a degree in marine biology.

"Why haven't I heard about any of this?"

The clock on the fireplace mantel ticked in time to the sound of dog nails crossing the wooden floor into the dining room. Comet had left the comfort of the oak fire and was now staring at me. Sandoz hid behind her like she had done something wrong. I could only sigh.

"Lindsey was afraid that you'd be disappointed in her." Freddie didn't bother to sugarcoat it. "She feels like she can't talk to you about these things. It'll either make you sick or mad." Sandoz and Comet split up, the golden pleading for Freddie's attention by hammering her elbow, the greyhound slowly sanding my hand, which had fallen to my side. Freddie struck the last nail. "I think she's upset because you've never been to her campus for anything — not even

241

parents' days."

Panic swelled as this information sank in, and I broke out in a sweat.

"Are you all right?' Freddie was patting my face with a cotton napkin. "Your shirt is soaked."

"After I get back to Sedona, I need a ticket to Tampa."

It took an entire day for me to drive 120 miles from Sedona to Phoenix in order to spend a night resting at my mom's house. The flight to Tampa was four hours, much longer than my usual flights between Phoenix and Omaha. I arrived late on a Friday night, Comet helping wheel and support me for more than two hours while we negotiated through a nearly empty concourse and commuted to the hotel. Lindsey was neither ecstatic nor unhappy to see me.

"Hi, Dad," she said, but her smile didn't reach her eyes. "Do you want to see the campus first or my dorm room?" Her lackluster tone reminded me of how I used to sound when hosting out-of-town guests who had stayed too long at the lake house. I had been hoping for more fire from Lindsey, even an angry tirade — some evidence of her desire that I once again become emotionally invested in her life. But Lindsey's demeanor signaled that her own expectations of this visit were nil. Regardless of what did not occur, I spent most of Saturday upright and in her presence. I told her I loved her. Then I flew back to Phoenix. Comet was with me every step of the way, never leaving my side except when the hotel staff fought over who got to walk her at night.

I knew the girls were growing up and that many children distance themselves from their parents, at least for the first few years they're living away from home. I had been certain that my daughters were also avoiding me because they couldn't deal with my physical decline. Now I wondered if it had always been more complicated than that. Who was avoiding whom? Lindsey clearly thought I had been negligent. At least Kylie and Jackie would answer my calls, but even after my visit, Lindsey didn't respond to my efforts to stay in touch. I didn't like it, but I thought I understood. She needed to protect herself. Maybe she had felt abandoned by me once too often.

PART III

13

Four Years Later
Winter–Spring 2005 — Arizona

All the main rooms of our new house in Sedona had picture windows that framed Lee Mountain. From my recliner I could watch its planes and ridges turn orange, mint, violet, and vermillion as the quiet hours passed. Bright, billowing clouds that cast shadows as big as the mountain drifted overhead, then moved down the valley. It was exactly the kind of place where Freddie and I had always dreamed of retiring.

Freddie had moved to Sedona, however, not because we were retiring but because we could no longer afford two homes. My doctors had made it clear that I couldn't move back to Nebraska full-time, and our savings were gone. We sold the lake house, to the dismay of our daughters, who lost their childhood home. We also sold the little stucco house in Sedona and used the money

247

from both places to buy another home just a block away. This one was better suited to someone who used a walker and might soon be in a wheelchair. The house had the view, and it even had a swimming pool, which I could use for physical therapy.

It took us a year to sell both houses and buy the new one. During that time, as soon as I trained Comet to help me with one task, some other formerly trivial activity would slip beyond my grasp. I couldn't pull the sheets down when I needed to get out of bed, so I taught Comet to tug them off me. The only pieces of clothing I could place on my body without assistance were hats and shirts, so I used mechanical grabbers to hoist up my pants while I leaned on Comet for balance. Thank goodness for slip-on shoes.

Taking a shower was fraught with peril, even though the door was extra wide and opened both ways for easy access. Shortly after moving in, I made the mistake of falling to the shower floor. Comet heard my cussing thump and left her warm spot in bed to check out the commotion. Running over to the shower door, she pushed against it, banging the glass off my head. She continued to push, trying to gain entry, but instead the door squashed me against the shower wall.

"Comet! Back off. Or to the side. Go over there!" I couldn't think of the right words. Eventually she moved away, giving me space to swing the door open and crawl onto the bathroom tile.

I soon taught Comet to open the shower door by pulling on a bath towel I hung on the handle. After a few more spills she was an accomplished lifeguard, allowing me to grasp her collar while she dragged me out of the shower. At first, the sight of her drenched, whiskered face staring down at me like a seal looking at a fish made me laugh. As my condition worsened, that same face, dripping with concern, would prompt me to soothe her, "It's all right, Comet. I can't drown in an inch of water."

When Freddie first moved to Sedona, she tried to lure me out of the house to explore the local galleries, restaurants, and clubs. She wanted to visit Ben Wright's studio and watch him work, as I had. Friends who had gotten to know us as a couple during Freddie's earlier stays were eager to have us over. I rarely felt up for any of it. Time and again Freddie had to decline invitations, except for a few events she attended alone. Even our former neighbors and good friends Bill and Jana kept their distance, not wanting to intrude. Though Freddie repeatedly asked if we could just have them over for a drink, I was too tired for small talk. Besides, even in informal settings, my panic attacks soaked me within seconds of conversing with anyone other than Freddie.

I could still muster circling a few blocks with Comet. I usually managed by using my canes and Comet for support, but more and more frequently I clipped Comet's leash to a walker. I don't know which of us hated that contraption more. When she saw me going to get it, Comet would move just far enough away to force me to drag the walker over to her. As I approached she would stealthily take one small step forward, always staying just out of reach. When my rumblings became more heated, she would finally allow the walker to be clipped to her leash. But she would angrily avert her head, making sure I understood just how embarrassed she was by this pathetic rig.

Freddie had resigned from her position as head of the cardiac unit in Lincoln that she had founded eight years earlier. We didn't think she would be able to find a comparable position anywhere near Sedona, and we were right. After a few months of being my handyman, maid, housekeeper, and full-time nurse, Freddie had announced that she was changing professions. The only growth industry in Sedona was real estate, particularly resort time-shares. Freddie didn't know a thing about real estate, but she took a three-week course that taught her enough to pass Arizona's real estate exam and get a license to sell resort properties.

Most days Freddie worked ten-hour shifts at her new job. The time-share agents she was friendly with took full advantage of Sedona's many film festivals, jazz festivals, and other cultural events, and I was relieved when Freddie joined them. It made me feel a little less guilty. It also made up for the downside of her job, such as dealing with skeptical strangers who were only at a time-share presentation for the free helicopter ride. The stress was compounded by the fact that there wasn't a regular paycheck, only a commission on sales. Freddie's workweek no longer ended with Friday night; Saturday and Sunday were the heart of her schedule because that's when the buyers were in town. She had to be available any time a client was ready to sign documents.

After a quick night out commiserating with fellow salespeople over drinks, Freddie often came home to a dark house and a golden retriever craving attention. She had little time and less energy to catch up on daily household tasks and help care for a sick husband. Sweaty sheets were stacked faster than my clumsy cleaning attempts could keep up with. Clean laundry stayed in the washer because I couldn't reach down to pull the items out. Clean dishes remained in the dishwasher for the same reason. Because of depression and, now, panic attacks, I had once again been prescribed a regimen of medications that was far beyond my feeble ability to track. Freddie was in charge of that as well. Sandoz missed Freddie's comforting body next to the fireplace and became increasingly despondent despite my attempts to console her. Or maybe she was just hungry. I couldn't feed Comet or Sandoz because I couldn't reach their dishes or place them on the floor, so the moment my wife walked in she was rushed by two ravenous dogs.

Comet had by now assumed the additional duties of guard dog. At periodic intervals throughout the day she would patrol the house, staring outside to the front and back yards from various windows and glass doors. When I asked her to relax, she would ignore me. If someone was in our front yard, she would run to my side and stare, her version of a bark. She had developed the ability to sense when I was about to have an attack of muscle spasms and would force me into the nearest chair before they occurred. I didn't resent the help, but I did think that Comet's superior attitude — standing in front of me and staring like she couldn't believe my stupidity — was a little annoying.

Comet began her morning shift after Freddie left for work. She would leap onto my bed, her whining bugle and excited eyes telling me it was *time to get up, time to get up!* She was usually able to rouse me for a walk. We left Sandoz at home to snooze in the backyard or mope inside, waiting for Freddie to return.

For years Comet and I had ventured around a three-block area of the neighborhood. Comet had always intuitively known that she should walk close to me, and over time she improvised her own methods of protecting me. One of her favorite strategies was to turn her head toward me and extend her muscled rear end in the direction of any stranger who approached without warning. By placing her body between me and the intruder, she could prevent me from getting bumped. Now, when Comet and I went for a walk, she assumed the casual yet hyperalert demeanor of a professional bodyguard.

One afternoon when the neighborhood

was deserted, Comet and I went out for a stroll. As usual I was bent over my canes, for all intents and purposes no taller than a little old lady. Comet was acting spastic — walking a short distance, stopping with ears perked straight up, and then repeating the process. I strained to hear what she heard, but I caught only a faint rustling sound in the dried leaves beneath a row of shrubs. Then, out of nowhere, the shrubs spit a bushel of leaves at us. A skinny black and white dog exploded from the middle of the mess and rocketed straight at me. Without a bark or growl, the English pointer launched his attack directly at my face. I crooked my arm over my eyes, losing a cane and my balance simultaneously. As my arms flew out to break my fall, I saw Comet spring between the pointer and me. The pointer bounced off the asphalt, then spun back toward us with its teeth bared. Comet rushed to where I lay helpless on my back and stayed next to me, bracing herself. For the next three minutes — 180 agonizing seconds — Comet sacrificed her fierce inclination to fight back, stubbornly placing her body between the crazed dog and me. I was forced to watch as Comet's face repeatedly contorted in pain from the pointer's slashing bites, her chilling cries sounding nearly human. My mind howled at my body, *Do something! ANYTHING!* I snatched the end of one of my heavy wooden walking sticks and lashed out at the pointer's head. Several heavy cracking thuds told me I had hit my mark — the attacker vanished in a stream of yelps.

Comet collapsed in a whining pile onto the chilly asphalt. Years of lethargy vanished in an instant, and I managed to coordinate enough muscles to roll to my side and firmly seize the cane I had used to clobber the pointer. I pushed my lazy body across the grainy asphalt to Comet's side. "It's okay, girl. It'll be okay." I tried to remain calm as blood poured from jagged wounds in Comet's chest and flanks, her eyes rapidly rolling in fear and pain. "Damn it!" I wasn't cursing the other dog, not yet. I was screaming at my flaccid muscles, trying to inspire them to action. I groaned as I hoisted my body off the ground and, hand over hand, pulled myself up the walking stick. I couldn't have cared less about the searing pain that ripped through my lower back muscles, scorching my legs and feet. I had to get up and get help! *Now!*

Finally I grasped the top of my cane and clung to it, upright but dazed and moaning from the pain. It was precisely at that point that my best friend — the beautifully gentle greyhound who had just risked her life to save me from a vicious assault — forever sealed her throne in my heart. As she watched my clumsy effort to maintain balance, Comet tapped into some incredibly powerful spirit, yelping as she struggled to maneuver her rear legs beneath her. Slowly, shakily, and with small whimpering cries, Comet raised herself from the street. Shivering and slightly stumbling, she walked to my side and offered her assistance.

I hadn't wept in a long, long time, having given it up as a useless and energy-taxing activity. Now, in the middle of an empty street, banged up, covered with dirt, and balancing on one stick and a bloody dog, the tears gushed and I let them flow.

In a few minutes I collected myself enough to call Freddie's office from my cell phone. I looked up and down the block, but there was nobody around to help. Yet after what I had just witnessed, I'm not sure I would have accepted assistance anyway. Asking for help would have been an insult to Comet, who limped along next to me, absorbing my weight when I couldn't balance without her support. The blood from her wounds glistened in streaks of red and dark purple and dripped down her chest onto the pavement.

Tears dripped from my chin onto my sweat-soaked shirt. Blood and tears muddled along a step at a time. Yet I found myself *wanting* to stumble in step with Comet, proud to be included as a member of her personal fife and drum corps. This dog had more courage and integrity than a platoon of people like me. Twenty minutes and one block later, we fell through the front door into the living room.

Freddie immediately left work when the receptionist gave her my message. She loaded Comet into the back of the SUV and turned to me. "Stay here. It'll take too long to get you into the truck. Call the vet and tell them I'll be there in fifteen minutes." Freddie was locked into serious medical mode; that drive took twenty minutes on a good day.

Later that night, Comet gingerly adjusted her position on the fireside dog bed, her bandages oozing salve. Sandoz watched from the nearby floor, unsure about what had happened but giving support nonetheless. Despite Comet's obvious discomfort and the ferocity of the battering, she didn't act frightened or spooked. Instead, she watched me adoringly as I told Freddie about the attack. People who live with rescued racers often describe "the look," a gaze that makes you feel as if you're wrapped in warm, tender kindness. It's the sort of look a mother bestows upon her newborn. That was the expression on Comet's face as I fumed, "What the hell have those people done to that pointer to make him so mean?"

"Wolfie, you need to calm down," Freddie said soothingly.

"You can't own a high-energy dog like that and not give it lots of exercise. I've never seen anybody walk or even play with that dog!" Usually when I yelled, Comet would come over and stand until I petted her, almost always prompting a quieter dialogue. The fact that now she couldn't even get up from her bed made me whack the nearest chair with one of my canes. "I'm going over there! Those people need to know what they've done to my dog!"

Rather than pleading, "Stop! You can't go over there! Please, oh please." Freddie stifled a laugh.

"What?" I demanded.

She walked across the room and squeezed my cheeks until I was making a fish face. "I'm sorry. It's just that the vision of you dressed like that" — Freddie gestured at my saggy bathrobe — "ringing the neighbor's doorbell . . ." She coughed two more short laughs. Then, as quick as a spring shower, she changed into Miss Logic. "We're not letting this slide. Let's call the animal control people and file a complaint. They can handle it. Comet needs you here."

Although cracking the neighbors over the head with a walking stick still seemed like the best option, I didn't feel as if I was betraying Comet by resisting that urge. Strangely, I was energized by my new role as *her* nurse. Freddie coaxed Comet onto the bed, where she reclined for the next ten days, leaving only for short potty breaks. Some of her bites couldn't be stitched, so they required regular applications of new salve and gauze. The lacerations that were sutured started itching. Because I wouldn't make Comet wear the oversized cardboard collar that restricted her head movements, I needed to constantly stop her from licking the stitches.

Comet recovered with no obvious ill effects. Although she alertly monitored the barking from that particular yard, she once again displayed remarkable equanimity in the face of hardship. Life resumed as if nothing had happened. Taking my cue from Comet, I eventually walked to the neighbor's house and managed to explain passionately, but without resorting to violence, that Comet was not only my service dog, she was my dog, period. Animal control had been alerted to the situation. And before I left, I wanted them to know that there shouldn't be a next time. "If this ever happens again, the noose you find on your step won't necessarily be for your dog." The couple smiled at my comment, expecting me to laugh at my own joke. I didn't. It was almost as effective as one of my walking sticks.

When Comet was well enough, we resumed our regular routine. One day about a month after the attack, she was especially persistent about her morning walk. Jumping onto the bed, she stood over me, whining and drumming her paws on the mattress. "Not now, Comet." She hopped off but was back in five minutes. My eyes remained closed and I commanded, "Lie down next to me. We'll go in a minute."

Not a chance. Comet stood over me and bugled again. This time I opened my eyes. "Go get Mama. She's home, she'll walk you." I closed my eyes to the bright window shades. The bedsheets started shaking. My eyes flew open and there was Comet, chewing the corner of the bedcovers, her eyes directly focused on mine in challenge.

"Don't even think about it! If you pull these covers off, the only reason I'll get up is to flog you with your stuffed rabbit."

Comet pulled the corner of the sheets into her mouth, pawing them into submission with rapping front feet. The message was clear. *Get up or you'll have to punish me — that is, if you can get your fat butt up fast enough to catch me.* She definitely had my attention; I wanted to strangle her. Why, on this day with Freddie in the house and willing to walk her, did she totally refuse to heed my wishes?

Comet continued her strange behavior after she had dragged the covers from my body and helped me dress. I kept my canes by the front door, but today I was too tired to deal with them. Instead, I grabbed the detestable walker. Comet stood still, allowing me to clip her leash to it without a bit of resistance. I was so astonished that I didn't even praise her. I nearly looked over the door for a bucket of water: she had to be up to something.

We exited the house to glorious spring warmth that stirred the air but hadn't yet penetrated the ground and pavement. Neighborhood noises were comfortably muted, almost as if people didn't want to disturb Mother Nature's mood so early in the year. Comet carefully pulled ahead one or two steps at a time, allowing me to soak in the red-reflected beauty and tangy pine scent. The radiance of the day swept me into an expansive mood. Comet was in high spirits, too. Her horizontal ears perked sideways as she noted even the smallest changes in neighboring yards. Her bunny fur sparkled, vivid cinnamon separating glazed black tiger stripes. She was extra curious about every small movement in the dried pine needles and tree leaves, stopping frequently to sniff and poke at them with her long snout.

If not for our heightened senses, Comet and I would have passed by the unfamiliar couple the way we usually did with everyone except close neighbors — silently, making no eye contact. Instead, Comet made the rare effort to cross the street to investigate the strangers, heading straight for the large red-faced man. I pulled back on the walker, tugging Comet's head away.

"Comet, slow down! I'm sorry; she hardly ever just walks up to somebody she doesn't know."

A short blond woman was hovering behind the man, her eyes fixed on Comet.

"That's okay. We like dogs," the man said genially. He stuck out his hand. "Hi. My name is Bob. This is Arlene."

I was hoping he understood that I couldn't shake his proffered hand without risking my balance. "Nice to meet you both. This is Comet. Sorry about her rushing right up to you, but she's as gentle a dog as you'll ever meet." I directed the last comment at Arlene, who still hadn't emerged from behind her husband.

"Oh, don't worry about it. Do you live around here?" Bob was obviously a man who liked to take charge of the conversation. Arlene remained quiet, clinging to Bob's side and staring down at Comet, who was still as a stone. Before I could answer his question, he popped another one. "Do you know who lives at that house on the corner?" He gestured at my home.

"Yes." I wasn't about to tell a stranger where I lived.

Several seconds of silence passed while Bob smiled at me in anticipation. I remained quiet, so he filled the gap. "I was just wondering. I have a bronze eagle for sale that would look great on top of that outdoor fireplace." When I said nothing, Bob continued, "That's for another day anyway. So, what happened to you?"

Arlene dug her elbow into her husband's side. "Bob!"

I'll admit his question stunned me. People who encounter someone with an obvious disability very rarely acknowledge it. They divert their gaze, as if something interesting is going on near the horizon. Nervous sideways glances let the person with the unfortunate condition know that he's still included in the conversation. I was not prepared for anyone to be so forthright.

"Oh, I have a bad back," I replied.

Arlene looked bewildered, and Bob's expression was equally dubious. "Bad back? What do you mean bad back? It looks to me like you can hardly walk."

I couldn't help but laugh at his bluntness. "My spine sort of collapsed on itself — a lot of nerves are pinched and inflamed. It makes it hard for me to control my feet and legs. Just something that happened." My attempt to be flippant sounded hollow, but these were total strangers asking about a very intimate situation.

"Can't it be fixed?" Arlene's voice was soft and perplexed, as if she were talking to a foreigner who wasn't aware of the grand things that could be accomplished by health care in the United States.

I don't know why, but I started spilling the details. I explained the childhood years of pain and surgery. I described the lifetime of dealing with side effects I thought were normal. I told them about how the years of searching for solutions and failing to find a fix had ultimately brought me to that street on that day at that time. Comet was an integral part of the last pieces of my story.

When I was done, a shocked bubble of silence encompassed the four of us. Bob and Arlene took turns looking at Comet and then back to me. I suddenly felt awkward; I was embarrassed that my little story was so disturbing. "Well, I better finish with Comet's walk."

Arlene was petting Comet, the two of them now fully at ease with each other. She looked up at me and said simply, "We know somebody who can help you." Not probably. Not maybe. Not we can ask.

Bob jumped in with both feet. "We sure do. A friend of ours from Wisconsin retired here not long ago —"

This was Arlene's idea, and she wasn't about to let her husband steal the punch line. "His son is a physician's assistant for somebody who's a very skilled spinal surgeon. We'll call them and have Kai — that's their son's name, Kai Stobbe — get the doctor to call you."

The entire time from greetings to good-byes couldn't have taken more than ten minutes. But for some strange reason, I left the encounter with a good feeling. It wasn't because I expected anything to come of the talk. Countless times over the last several years some well-meaning person had suggested to Freddie or me that we investigate "this doctor who helped my daughter with her back," or "this chiropractor who can just move one bone and you're cured." We had been assured that "magical things can happen with Sedona energy vortexes," and even that "different light frequencies will make Wolf forget his pain." We had pursued so many different leads that it became a family joke. "Dad, have you tried pond scum? How about Botox to renew your spine? Have you contacted a faith healer or a medicine man?" Other than Botox and pond scum, I had. So when somebody told us that they knew about the best back doctor in the world, skepticism reigned.

"Wolfie, a doctor who is any good at all is too busy to just pick up the phone and call some guy who isn't even his patient." Freddie had listened to my description of the encounter, no doubt wondering why I thought this couple would have better information than what we had compiled over the years.

"I know that. I was just wondering if I

could somehow get the doctor's name and look him up on the Internet." The flicker of whatever I had felt when I talked to the couple was fading fast.

"Uh-huh." Freddie's tone extinguished the last ember.

So imagine my surprise when I stumbled to answer the phone a week later. "Could I speak to Mr. Steve Wolf, please?"

I was a little peeved. Our phone was on the Do Not Call list for telemarketers. "Can I tell him who's calling?"

"Yes. This is Kai Stobbe. My parents live in Sedona and —"

"Kai! This is Wolf . . . Mr. Wolf . . . Just call me Wolf."

An amused laugh echoed in my ear. "Hi, Mr. Wolf. As I said, my name is Kai. My parents called me a couple of days ago and told me that you have a horrible back condition. They looked up your phone number and wanted me to call you to see if the surgeon I work with might be able to help you."

14

March–June 2005 — Arizona

Freddie was due home from work in eight hours, and until then I nervously wobbled from room to room, out to the pool and back inside again. I knew she would try to douse my expectations, which surely could only lead to disappointment. Freddie paid her own mental toll every time I received another negative medical assessment. She would have to watch me absorb the blow, and of course anything that happened with my health impacted her future. Despite all this, I pounced the minute she walked in the door. "Would you call Kai back and find out what information they need to give an opinion?"

After almost thirty years in the medical profession, Freddie had special insight into this type of communication. She could glean important nuggets from any medical propaganda that might casually be mentioned to sway a patient. I didn't trust myself. I was at the point where I would either grab at any proffered straw or fail to recognize a legitimate opportunity.

Freddie's eyes sparkled when she hung up the phone. "I have to say that so far, I'm impressed. The fact that this office took the time to call a total stranger is unheard of. And this group appears to know what they're talking about. They're at the aggressive end of treatment." Her growing excitement was unusual. "You can tell that a doctor and his staff are passionate about what they do when they agree to take a look at your case without charging anything. All Kai wants are the latest MRIs and radiologist reports. If the images are detailed enough, he'll sit down with the surgeon and go over everything."

My body started to tingle. A pleasurable chill raced down my arms. "Who are these guys, anyway?"

Freddie opened her laptop and murmured, "Colorado Comprehensive Spine Institute . . . Dr. George A. Frey . . . Let's see . . ."

Starting with the caveat, "Everything looks better on paper," Freddie later reported her findings. "Frey is an orthopedic spine surgeon who founded the Spine Institute.

269

He went to med school at Georgetown in DC, and his residency and fellowship were at St. Luke's in Chicago."

"Is that good?" Like most people, I didn't know which medical schools specialized in which areas, but Freddie did.

She nodded. "It's really good. According to Dr. Frey's bio, he 'completed advanced specialized training in reconstructive and traumatic spinal surgery involving all regions of the spine.' He isn't the typical back doctor who only works on the lower lumbar region."

Hope was still a small island in a vast ocean, but it felt good to think about sailing in that direction. "Their office is in Englewood, a suburb on the south edge of Denver," Freddie continued, and I piped up, "One of my clients told me Denver is a big hub for spine-related work."

A week after my medical records were forwarded, I started marking days like a prisoner. I forced myself to stay awake so that I could pester Freddie at night about her conversation with Kai: "Did he say if he'd call or was he going to mail a report back to us? Should I call him and find out? Should I schedule an appointment?" I think Freddie started staying out later with her friends in the hope that I would be asleep before she got home. Comet, however, was delighted with my impatience. I was so fidgety in the morning that I eagerly awaited her leaping request for a walk. She got an extra mini outing when I asked her to pull the blankets off me so I could make it to the mailbox in time to talk to our rural mail carrier.

When I wasn't obsessing about the mail, I was calculating whether it would be my cell or the home phone that would bring the news from Dr. Frey's office. But when the spine institute number finally flashed on the handset, I couldn't pick up the phone. As much as I had tried to prepare myself, I wasn't sure I was strong enough for bad news. Maybe it would be easier to screen the call and listen to the information without having to respond. I lay in bed, tensely waiting for the recorder to click on. Just as it did, I remembered that medical providers don't leave this type of private message on an answering machine. "Hello, Mr. Wolf. This is Kai Stobbe calling. You can reach me later today or tomorrow morning at —"

I pressed the speaker button. "Hey, Kai. How are you?" Comet plopped her head on my chest, watching me talk.

"Busy but good. How have you been do-ing?" Kai actually sounded as if he was interested.

"Couldn't be better," I said lightly.

"We received your information, and Dr. Frey has reviewed the records. He also talked to the other doctors here to get their opinions." The long preamble was not a good sign. I was familiar with the beginning of a gentle letdown.

"It's that bad, huh?"

The line was quiet for several seconds. "Yeah, it is. Your back's a mess, but you already knew that."

After all this time, I thought I was over the hurt. Instead, my bowels flipped and I felt like I was going to faint. A harsh buzzing filled my ears. "Yes, I know my back's a mess. Still, it's never pleasant to hear it."

"I'll bet." Kai paused. "The good news is that Dr. Frey thinks he can help you."

I shook my head so hard trying to clear out the bees that Comet lifted her head from my chest and stared, ears pointed at the ceiling.

"What?"

Kai's voice became louder, as if he thought we had a bad connection. "I said that Dr. Frey thinks he can at least significantly reduce your pain. I was calling to set up a time when you could talk with him. From the look of these films, I doubt that you could drive up here for a visit."

I couldn't react. Instead, I felt oddly detached from the situation, as if I were eavesdropping on a party line. The news was too good; there had to be a loophole. "Sure," I said, in the clinically cool tone of someone who did this for a living. "But could I call you back? Freddie will want to be in on the conversation, too."

"Of course. I'm going to mail you a brief report along with the films, which have been marked to show you some of the problems. That way you'll have a better idea of what the doctor will be discussing with you."

After turning off the speaker, the conversation receded into the deep background. Not another thought about what had just transpired entered my head. I stared at the bedroom television until I heard Freddie come home. When she walked into the bedroom, her slumped shoulders and tired eyes told me how hard her day must have been. She shuffled over to the closet, shedding her jacket and kicking off her shoes.

"Kai called. He wants us to call him," I said blandly.

Freddie's head spun around so fast I thought we might need an exorcist. "He called? What did he say?"

"He wants to set up a time for us to have

a phone conversation with Frey."

"About what? Wolfie, what did Kai tell you?"

"He said they think they can help me." My eyes were fixed on the television. I didn't offer any more details.

"Wha— I mean, what did he . . . How? I need to know everything Kai said. Everything from hello to good-bye. Don't just sit there like a dead mummy, tell me!"

"He said that the doctor, and I quote, 'thinks he can at least significantly reduce your pain. I was calling to set up a time when you could talk with him' — unquote."

Freddie sat on the bed and grabbed my hand. "Wolfie! That's great news! Aren't you excited?"

My first impulse was to tell the truth — I wasn't sure. I revised that thought as I watched Comet react to Freddie's sudden zing by standing on the mattress and nuzzling her cheek. "Let's just see what this whiz-kid doctor has to say."

We received Kai's package and set up a conference call with Dr. Frey. I was immediately struck by the doctor's warm, confident tone and good humor. It was rare to encounter a physician who gave the impression that he was in no hurry and had all day to answer your questions. I later found out that this wasn't an act. Dr. Frey believed in defusing fears of the unknown and reducing anxiety that might interfere with a successful outcome.

He also believed in assigning his patients homework. Dr. Frey told me to research every item on the report they had sent, including my current condition and the multifaceted operation they were proposing. Frey ended the conversation with, "You have a host of problems that make the results unpredictable, but I'm confident that I can reduce your pain. I can't cure you, but I can help you. Get back to Kai after you do your homework, and let us know if you want to go forward."

My homework list was extensive, an indication of the complexity of my medical condition. Rather than feeling overwhelmed, however, I attacked my assignment with all the intensity I had once applied to high-stakes legal cases. First I examined Dr. Frey's assessment of my current condition. My existing fusion would soon be thirty-five years old, and the bone that had been placed along the two moving vertebrae had gone wild, partially attaching to levels higher than originally intended. I now had instability affecting spinal nerves from L3 (the third lumbar disc space) to my sacrum.

Every lumbar disc was dehydrated and misshapen, causing instability and narrowing of the spinal canal throughout my entire lower back, a condition known as stenosis. The sway, or curve, that most people have in their lower back was totally absent because of all the other damage. My back was as straight as a fence post, which meant that my spine was mercilessly hammered directly into my pelvis.

To help ease the pain from these interconnected problems, Dr. Frey would begin with an anterior lumbar interbody fusion. It was basically a modified gutting procedure. The patient is filleted from the front with a long slice starting below one side of the rib cage and continuing to the belly crease at the waist. Vital organs are moved out of the way and the spine is exposed. Tissue that is blocking access to the spine is dissected. Then the patient's body is bent so far backward that the spine pops forward into the abdominal cavity for better visualization, and a flood of blood and dissected tissue is vacuumed. The goal of all this is to clear the way for implanting threaded fusion cages.

Threaded fusion cages are porous miniature thimbles filled with tiny shredded pieces of bone and sponges that contain bone morphogenetic protein, or BMG. Two of these cages are placed in the disc space of each level that is to be fused. BMG helps keep the bone alive and promotes bone growth so that the new bone tissue will attach to the adjacent vertebrae, which have been scraped to bleed so the tissue more readily adheres. Eventually that part of the spine grows into one stable piece. In my case this would have to be done at five separate disc spaces, but only after what was left of each bad disc was sucked up like useless fish guts.

That was one part of the procedure. I would also be having a posterior spinal fusion, which involved "segmental pedicle screw instrumentation." The doctor would perform this approaching the spine from the back rather than the front. Dr. Frey would also scrape, sand, and dissect in and around the bones and nerves, then create a "bed" at each affected level, where more bone and BMG would be placed. After cleaning up the old fusion, decompressing the facet nerves on each vertebra, and freeing nerves in other passageways, wedges would be cut into the vertebrae. These wedges were similar to the ones foresters chop into trees to get them to fall in the right direction. Titanium screws would be implanted in the vertebrae so that two curved titanium rods could be attached, restoring proper spine curvature. While my spine would then have the proper lordotic curve, it would be permanently fused into that shape, one solid mass that would not bend or "articulate" back and forth like a normal back. There was something ironic about the medical profession giving a plaintiff's lawyer a stronger backbone, but who was I to put up a fuss about semantics?

While I was completing my homework, Freddie was doing research of her own. I knew we were reading from different material when she started scrutinizing the risks involved. "I can't imagine that all this could be done in one procedure. And repeated surgeries increase your risks without increasing the odds of a good result. Your current doctors are already worried about your physical condition. I don't know what they'd say about subjecting you to several surgeries."

"Freddie, you're talking three or four hours at most. I don't think he'd have any problem doing it all in one surgery."

Freddie laughed. "Wolfie. It takes that long just to fix a hernia."

During our follow-up conversation with Dr. Frey, he assured us that all the work could be done in a single surgery, possibly with more than one surgical team. But it would take much longer than four hours — how long, they couldn't tell. It depended on the extent of the damage they found after I was filleted. Rehabilitation could take some time because of the years of nerve damage and pain, coupled with atrophied muscles that had compensated along different nerve pathways for most of my life.

After this conversation I wasn't exactly ecstatic, but I was resolute. "Freddie, I say we do this. What choice do I have? If we don't take this chance I may be dead before the next one comes along."

To my surprise, Freddie was more enthusiastic. "It sounds like he can fix a lot of what's wrong. Wouldn't that be great? We might even go back to being a normal boring couple."

We scheduled the surgery for August 5. That would give us time to trek back to Omaha in late May for Kylie's graduation from law school. While there, I would be able to visit my regular doctors and learn what I would need to do to get healthy enough for the operation. I would also have an opportunity to see Lindsey, who was now happily enrolled in a bachelor's degree nursing program in Omaha, far away from any ocean.

Not wanting to detract from Kylie's big day, we had not yet told the girls about my surgical plans. The graduation ceremony passed in a haze. I was there, but I wasn't, at once fantasizing about the future and falling back into the past. Now twenty-five, Kylie had been sixteen when I collapsed on the basketball court. She and I were similar in so many ways, from looks to logic to passion. Her decision to become an attorney made me feel as if I had passed something of value on to her. Sitting in the audience that day, however, I wondered how many of my not-so-wonderful traits Kylie and the other girls had absorbed. By refusing to acknowledge the extent of my problems and insisting on handling them by myself, I had alienated the people I loved the most. The whole time the girls were growing up, I had never allowed them to see me in a moment of weakness — until it all came crashing down. My behavior since then had often been baffling even to myself. I vowed that someday I would sit down with my daughters and ask them how they had felt about this whole long saga. But today I just hugged Kylie, told her, "I am beyond proud of you," and stood up as straight as I could for the family photos after the ceremony.

The doctors in Omaha, with whom I had worked for years, advised me on how to prepare for the upcoming surgery. One concern was that I would be banking my own blood, which, thanks to my diet, was pretty much like liquid bacon. I never had gotten healthier in my eating habits. I would need medication to tame the cholesterol levels, a good diet, and other drugs to get the nerve inflammation down. I also was instructed to "do whatever you can, no matter how little, to help get your body in better condition before the surgery."

At those words, the triathlete in me perked back to life. Swimming, cycling, running — yes! I could do some version of that. On the return flight to Phoenix, I started to outline my planned regimen to Freddie. "Each morning I'll swim for an hour, then hike with Comet. And I have my old weights and lifting equipment stored in the garage."

"Steve, please get those ideas out of your head. Just getting healthy enough to tread water for ten minutes would be a huge improvement. You don't need a marine boot camp."

But I was on a mission. The day after we arrived back in Sedona I plunged into the pool and within two minutes had to be fished out by Freddie as I frantically struggled to keep my head above water. The next day I attempted to walk around the neighborhood without the help of Comet or canes. I lasted a half block and it felt like several thousand kilometers. The following morning I was glued to the mattress like roadkill.

"Imbécile," I thought I heard Freddie mumble, and then, "What good is exercise if it causes so much pain that you can't get out of bed for the next two days?" Her voice was a monotone but her eyes burned with frustration.

Compared to the last two days, a week-long binge on questionable muscatel would have been a vacation. "Maybe I should take it a little easier?"

"You think?" I felt Sandoz tense at Freddie's tone. Comet had already retreated to the adjacent room. Freddie continued, "I have to leave for work. I was going to have the pool drained, but if you think that more than two of your brain cells are now working, we can tell the pool guy we don't need him — yet."

As the weeks unfolded, we found ourselves laughing at the very thought of draining the swimming pool. The summer was shaping up to be one of the hottest on record. Despite the increasing heat, Comet never lost her enthusiasm for accompanying me on our walks, which slowly became longer and more frequent. It was during one of our early afternoon strolls that Comet once again demonstrated her extraordinary courage and devotion, not to mention a very strong stomach.

I had finally conquered the short hill leading from our house to an elevated series of lots that offered a spectacular view of the nearby rock monuments. Through a thick corridor of juniper, manzanita shrubs, and prickly pear cactus, a narrow dirt trail wound to the top of the hill. Over its crest, a gravel road led back to the neighborhood. The total walk was less than three-quarters of a mile, but the changes in elevation and the uneven dirt trail were as much of a challenge as I needed. Today, the oppressive heat added to the toll.

"Let's take a rest, Comet," I wheezed at the top of the hill. I found a seat on a boulder while Comet investigated some nearby javelina droppings that were tinted the same bright purple as the prickly pear fruit. When I finally caught my breath, I urged Comet forward. "Okay, girl, time to go cool off at home." The pathway tapered to single file. I was tired, my legs shaking from assuming the main duty of balancing on my burning feet. The paved roadway was less than a football field ahead, and I was determined to make it there without another rest. Comet was walking directly in front of me so that I could use her back for balance, when suddenly she stopped in the middle of the path.

"Come on, Comet. Let's go. I'm tired." She wouldn't budge, instead tilting her head and lifting her nose at something I was unable to detect. "Let's go, girl. You can bark at the javelina tomorrow." Comet ignored me. Irritated and hot, I walked alongside her, wedging my body through the thick shrubbery. She refused to make room for me to get past. Instead, she looked up at me and whined. After being with this dog 24/7 for years by now, I knew her warning when I heard it, but it was too late. Squeezed onto the loose dirt and rocks at the edge of the trail, I lost my balance and fell backward into the bushes.

I wasn't really worried because I knew the thick shrubbery would cushion my fall. Sure enough, when I hit the ground it felt like I had been caught by a sponge — a loose, lumpy, sodden sponge that exploded into a repulsive, stinking cloud. I had landed in a foot-deep pile of rotting corpses, hundreds of rats and deer mice that someone had trapped and dumped along the trail.

I've been around a lot of wild animals and domestic livestock that have been gutted and cleaned for food, but I have never experienced such an appalling stench — putrefied rodents sautéed in the desert sun and left to rot in a giant heap of oozing entrails. And I could not get up. "Ayeeeeeeee! Ayeeeeeee!" I frantically thrashed, trying to push myself off of the decaying pile of rat, flinging guts and blood everywhere.

Comet's instincts had warned her of the danger. Those same senses were now shouting at her to flee, to get as far away from this mess as possible — there was disease here and she knew it. Not even the javelinas had disturbed this pile of crap. But instead of running, Comet slowly picked her way toward me through the gore — carefully, daintily, like a bride-to-be trying to protect an expensive pedicure. Her grimaced snarl, squinted eyes, and upturned nostrils were so humanly revolted that I stopped panicking and started to laugh.

Comet has never liked people laughing at her expense. I knew her feelings were hurt and she wanted to run away just to teach me a lesson. Yet she leaned down so I could grab her collar and then stepped backward, hauling me upright to my knees and letting me lean on her until I could stand. Comet's rear muscles popped as she pulled me from the sewage and onto the path.

I often think about what would have happened if Comet had fled or refused to enter the putrid pit. It was bad enough that I was in that stench as long as I was. Within hours of returning home, I started to have trouble getting enough air into my lungs. Soon after, my temperature began to climb and I got a horrible headache. By nightfall I couldn't stand without black dots from lack of oxygen dancing through my eyes. When my temperature hit 103 degrees, we went to the ER. They ruled out the flu and pneumonia and sent me home, in Freddie's care.

A week later I finally started to recover from what was likely a case of hantavirus, a pulmonary hemorrhagic virus humans contract from inhaling rodent urine and droppings. It can rapidly progress to life-threatening breathing problems. Without Comet I would have been stranded, breathing in that diseased stench for hours.

There is no effective treatment for hantavirus, but if you live through it, neither are there long-term side effects. Since I was banking blood for the upcoming procedure, this was good news. Freddie wasted no time in making the most of a teachable moment.

"This is what happens when you push yourself too hard. Now will you calm down?"

For once I listened. Besides, after all the excitement, Comet and I had decided that the perfect way to pass our time was sitting peacefully by the pool, with an occasional perambulation around the neighborhood by way of sidewalks. If my blood and body weren't strong enough to handle the operation by now, there wasn't much I could do about it. I just prayed that someday I would forget the odor of rotting rat carcasses. So far, I haven't.

In the days that followed, I kept waiting for Comet to regard me with the skepticism I deserved for ignoring her warning on the trail. What I got instead was her usual gaze of adoration and love. Apparently, when she had first chosen to come home with me from Flagstaff, she had fully expected that I would introduce her to a whole new world of weird.

True to form, when I told Comet that we had to go down to Scottsdale, into the Valley of the Sun — the very, very, very hot sun — she jumped into the back of the SUV as if she expected a visit to Santa's Workshop. That summer, our second without the respite of the lake house, was already an unrelenting scorcher. Just the thought of going to a lower, hotter altitude drained whatever reserves of good cheer Freddie and I had left, but Scottsdale was where I banked my blood for the surgery, so we had to drive there once a week.

As the SUV crept through an all-day traffic jam on the interstate that circled Scottsdale, we passed dozens of megamalls and shopping strips splayed alongside the highway. I thought about neutron bombs, how they make human beings pop like overinflated balloons but pass through buildings and cars without causing damage. In Scottsdale I saw buildings without one empty parking space and malls with armies of off-road vehicles, but no people. There was no one on the sidewalks, at the bus stops, or in front of the restaurants. At eleven o'clock in the morning it was 115 degrees.

When I opened the door to pull myself from the SUV, moisture evaporated from every cell in my body. The thick cushions that I wore inside my boots were hot after two steps on the asphalt, which shimmered with water mirages only a few meters from where we stood. Comet exited the truck as cool as a Kentucky Derby mint leaf, landing at my side without a flinch although blisters had to be forming on the bottom of her paws. "Freddie, please take Comet inside right away. You can come back and get me."

But despite Freddie's tugs on her leash, Comet didn't move. I took the leash from Freddie and slowly made my way toward the building's front door. Comet's paws had to be searing, yet step by step, she stayed by my side. There was a job to do, and Comet didn't have time for whining. I tried to follow her example, all the way to Denver.

15

August 2005 — Denver
On the third of August, Freddie, Comet, and I drove west for the surgery. My mom, her husband of two years, Manny, and my sister, Debbie, were going to meet us in Denver and stay for a few days after the surgery. The girls had wanted to come as well, but I talked them out of it. Instead, they were planning on a visit a month later, a point in my recovery when I thought I'd be bored to death and need the company.

"I hope you packed enough," Freddie said as we pulled out of the driveway. "It's hard not knowing how long you'll be there. And I don't know what I'm going to do; my boss wants me back in Sedona in a week, and if things don't go well, a week isn't . . ." Her voice caught, but before I could interrupt she held up her right hand, silencing me. When she spoke again, it was so softly that I thought she was talking to herself. "Kai said you would be staying no less than a month to six weeks, with the possibility of longer. Some of that time will probably be in a rehab facility, but still, that's pretty indefinite."

One of Freddie's sources of amusement over the summer had been my initial assumption that the operation would be only slightly more complex than a wisdom tooth extraction. The doctor's office had quickly set me straight on that. Still, I had my own ideas about rehab. The advantage I had over most patients was that I had been learning the tricks of managing a bad back my entire life. It was already second nature to get in and out of chairs properly, roll in and out of bed, bend at the knees, and sit and stand correctly. My muscles were weak, but they had worked so much overtime in years past that I was confident in their ability to pick up right where they had left off. Plus I had a secret weapon to help me — Comet. As for the pain, it couldn't get any worse.

"Let's plan on ten days for the hospital stay," I told Freddie. "After that, it's just a matter of where I'll be." I knew ten days sounded too brief, so I changed the subject. "I'll need to concentrate on recovery, so Comet should go home with you. Besides, Sandoz will miss her after a week with the neighbors." Freddie glanced over at me with slightly narrowed eyes.

In the hotel room Freddie confirmed our presurgery appointments for the next day. I was lying on my back on the bed, staring at the ceiling, when I noticed that the only sound in the room after she hung up was the air-conditioner fan. I turned my head and saw her looking at me. "What?" I asked.

"I'm just trying to decide what you're up to. You're being way too quiet."

"Freddie, I'm just mentally gearing up for a good result. After all we've been through, it's taking a bit of an effort to ratchet up my inner optimist."

"Uh-huh." Freddie regarded me skeptically. She was familiar with my belief that mentally preparing for a good result was as important as the physical preparation, a principle echoed by Dr. Frey. But prior to the fall at the YMCA, I had been blessed with speedy recoveries all my life. *If she gets even the slightest whiff that I want to be home within two weeks . . .*

The night before the surgery I didn't sleep. The closed eyes of a greyhound no longer fooled me; Comet was awake every moment as well. When I decided to shower at four in the morning, closing the bathroom door so that Freddie could slumber a little longer, Comet had irritatingly shoved the door open so she could keep an eye on Freddie from her position on the bath towel by the tub. Later Freddie filled her bowl with food, but Comet ignored it. When Freddie took her outside, Comet urinated on a bush next to the lobby door and immediately pulled Freddie back to our room.

Over the past year, Comet had displayed an uncanny ability to decipher speech and gestures that weren't even directed her way. She always knew when something unusual was going on with my health, and in those instances she refused to leave my side except for the briefest of breaks. Freddie had resorted to spelling words like *have to leave* or *go* or even *doctor,* to no avail. On this morning Comet had no patience for dallying on a walk. She wanted to know where I was and where we were going, *we* being the operative word.

At 5:30 a.m. we arrived at the hospital, and Comet conducted a nook-and-cranny inspection of all exits before allowing us to proceed to the admissions desk. She repeated the drill when we moved to the surgery waiting room, where my mom, Manny, and Debbie were already gathered.

"Hey!"

"Here we are!"

Stress was sparking like electricity among the anxious clan. Freddie sat down stiffly in a chair next to the doors to the surgical wing, clutching her luggage-size purse as if it were a life raft. My mom's face was etched with fatigue, her eyes red and swollen. I watched her nervously strike up a conversation with a nurse who was writing down the names of waiting family members. I had tried to leave Debbie out of the loop when it came to the details of my decline, but Mom kept updating her and she insisted on being here for the surgery. Watching my sister jiggle her leg while chattering to Manny, I realized how much she reminded me of Mom when she was younger.

I sat on the edge of a wing chair on the other side of the room. Because of the pre-surgery instructions not to eat or drink anything after midnight, it was better that I not linger next to the snack table with its warm donuts and freshly brewed coffee. But as always over the past five years, I wasn't alone. Comet sat quietly at my feet. As I had done hundreds of times before, I lost myself for a moment admiring her sculptural form, the rabbit-soft fur, the closed eyes and perked ears. It was impossible for me to think of any scenario that would have brought me to this hospital on this day if it were not for Comet and my wife. I wiped my eyes and scratched Comet's ears. "Enough of this. I'll have plenty of time to ruminate while I'm glued to a hospital bed." Comet helped me from the chair. The pastries were gone and I wanted to sit by Freddie.

"A penny for your thoughts. That's about all that'll be left by the time this spectacle is over."

Freddie ignored the joke. "The nurse will be here for you pretty soon. I've got Lindsey's phone number on speed dial so that you can call her right before you leave. It's her birthday and you said you wanted to call her today. Kylie gave me a phone number to call, too. And Jackie. Your mom looks tired and —" I put my arms around her, trying to stem the nervous prattle, and tears exploded down her face. I was already crying. We hung on to each other for several minutes before Freddie took a deep breath and said, "This kind of mood isn't going to help that old magical Wolfie mental state." She tried to smile, but her mouth just wouldn't turn upward.

At six thirty the door from the surgical wing to the waiting area opened. Freddie grabbed my arm, spinning me into a hug in front of the door. *"Je t'aime."* She was sobbing.

I was just an Iowa farm boy who had always hankered for somebody to whisper gooey French words into my ear. "Me, too."

I waved good-bye to everybody and left. Then, just for the hell of it, I reopened the door, knowing that Comet was still standing on the other side. "Comet, take care of the women until I get back." Freddie told me later that she could hear me laughing even after the door closed.

I left Comet to protect the family, but the greyhound had other ideas. She had planted herself on the floor directly in front of the double doors through which I had vanished, and now she was stretched to her full length, eyes shut, still as a stone. As soon as I was gone Freddie pulled Comet's leash from her purse. She badly needed to get out of there, decompress, and compose herself for what was going to be a very long day.

"Come on, Comet. Let's go for a walk."

Normally the word *walk* was jet fuel for a supersonic dash to the leash. This time Comet didn't even open her eyes. Freddie relented and waited a few more minutes. Several nurses and doctors pushed through the doors, only to shuffle sideways in order to avoid the cinnamon-striped dog stretched at their feet. Freddie repeatedly apologized to the surprised staff, who always responded, "That's okay, it's no problem." Then, "What kind of dog is that? She's beautiful." Comet refused to budge; flattery meant nothing to her today. She wouldn't even raise her head.

After a few of these interchanges, Freddie kneeled on the floor beside Comet and coaxed, "Come on, girl. We'll go outside for a walk and see if the bunnies are up yet." No response. "Comet, I know you have to finish with your potty business. Let's go." Still no movement or the slightest acknowledgment that Freddie was in the room. "We can get you a treat." Nothing. "Comet. I don't have time for this. Come on!"

Comet's head shot up and she pinned Freddie with a glare that warned, *Back off.* "She scared me," Freddie later confessed. "I decided to just leave her alone for a while."

In spite of the harried comings and goings of our family, other folks waiting in the lounge, and the hospital staff, Comet refused to leave the spot she had staked out. She had to be hungry, but she rejected the food and treats Freddie offered. She had to be uncomfortable because of her too-brief walk at 5:00 a.m., but she never uttered the short whine that signaled she needed a break. She had to be frustrated with the continual flow of traffic through the nearby door and the people who were forced to step directly over her, but she never moved a muscle. Comet didn't even flinch when someone would stumble into her as they pushed through the door.

Every hour a member of the surgical team would come out and tell the family how my operation was progressing. They eventually paid Comet no heed, stepping over her as if she were a familiar street curb. The updates were sometimes technical, but usually they were general assurances that the surgery was proceeding successfully and I was still breathing. Then, at approximately thirty minutes after noon, a nurse negotiated her way past Comet to Freddie with good news. "Dr. Frey has finished with the work from the front. Once that incision is sutured, he'll make his incision from the back and begin the work with the rods and cages. Mr. Wolf has tolerated the surgery very well and his vital signs are good." I had been in the operating room for six hours.

"How much longer?" asked my mom.

"We just don't know. We'll keep you

updated." She turned to go but stopped before stepping over Comet. "Has this dog even moved?"

The afternoon stretched into a routine of medical updates and small skirmishes pitting Comet's will against Freddie's fire. "Comet, you have to get up. I mean it! You can't go this long without relieving yourself!"

Comet remained totally still, eyes closed in annoyance, letting Freddie know that her threats were futile. When Freddie forced the collar past her snout and over her head, Comet shrugged out of it and shot Freddie another glare: *Leave me alone!*

"Fine, then! Just lie there and suffer!" Tense as Freddie was, she couldn't help but laugh as Comet turned her head and slowly, deliberately, lowered it to the floor.

Sometime around seven o'clock that night, twelve hours after I first entered surgery, Dr. Frey stepped over Comet and into the waiting room. Freddie hurried to meet him. As she skidded to a stop in front of the doctor, his face split into a wide smile. Before anyone could speak, Comet popped up from the floor and pushed herself between Freddie and the doctor, ears perked and laser eyes focused on Frey. Dr. Frey chuckled at the interference, then turned his attention to Freddie. "It was a challenge, but everything appears to have gone well. We had some unexpected obstacles, but nothing serious, just time-consuming. The nurses are cleaning your husband up and he should be in the recovery room soon. He'll be there awhile. It was a long surgery."

Freddie wiped her cheeks. "Well, what do you think?"

"He appears to have tolerated the surgery very well. Several of his major nerves, including both sciatic nerves, were seriously entrapped, but they've been freed up now. If nothing else, his pain should be reduced." Dr. Frey returned Freddie's hug before heading back into the surgical area. Over his shoulder he called, "The staff told me that Comet parked herself in front of this door and refused to move the whole time. Wow!"

The room had been stretched to its bursting point all day by the adrenaline and stress. Once the door closed, the tribe that had gathered around Freddie during the doctor's report looked at one another for a happy, stunned moment and let out a collective sigh. The walls and furnishings regained their original shapes, more real and less threatening. Everybody was exhausted, so the subdued celebration that followed lasted only ten minutes. It was unanimously agreed that a nice meal was in order since I wouldn't be conscious for a few more hours.

As the family collected their belongings in the now-deserted waiting room, Freddie rummaged through her purse for Comet's leash. She turned to the spot in front of the doors to the surgery wing. "Com . . . where's Comet?" Between the tears, hugs, and congratulations that had just transpired, no one had noticed that Comet was gone.

"She didn't leave with the doctor did she?" asked my mom. The rest of the family stood glued to the floor, looking around as if they expected Comet to pop out from behind one of the small chairs.

Freddie hustled to the door leading to the main hospital corridor, calling, "Comet! Here, girl. Come here, Comet." Seeing no sign of her, Freddie sprinted down the hall and around the corner leading to the elevators. Just like the first time in Sedona, when I had questioned Comet's ability to find her way home, the greyhound was standing in sharp profile in front of the elevator doors, her head tilted mockingly, as if to ask Freddie, "What took you so long?"

Freddie later told me that Dr. Frey's appearance had been like a hypnotist snapping his fingers. When the doctor had smiled with his good news, Comet instantly switched out of her intense, trancelike vigil and transformed back into the unflappable, independent spirit we recognized. She didn't even object when Freddie left her in the hotel room while the family went to dinner. Apparently Comet had concluded that all was well.

My surgery and recovery time had taken up the entire day and night of Thursday. By Friday evening my body started to register the train wreck I had been in. Before the actual operation, I had anticipated that the initial postsurgery pain would be due to the incision from my front rib cage to my waist. If not the stomach, I assumed that the area along my spine, from just below my shoulder blades to my tailbone, might fire off jolts of pain wherever a rod or cage had been inserted. Instead, my first discomfort was from neither of those areas. An aching throb and burning stabs radiated from the muscles in my midback around to my front ribs.

"What's wrong?" Freddie had been stationed at my bedside in the ICU for most of the day, but because my tongue and mind still hadn't fully synchronized, I hadn't said a word to her. Now she saw me grimace and warned, "Wolfie, you are not going to pull that macho-macho routine this time. If you're in pain, the nurses need to know so they can get you something. What's wrong?"

"Smy bhhoth," I mumbled.

"What?" I could tell that Freddie was trying not to giggle. She had the wide-eyed look of innocence, but her lips twitched like a cat's.

"Smiiii buuth . . ." My words were longer but no more intelligible. I lifted my right hand a few inches from the blanket. "Ubth thah!"

Freddie's giggles started as a soft huff, but squeals soon took full possession of her. She held her hand up, signaling that she was trying to stop. But I didn't want her to; the sound was wonderful. Then my laughter, still hoarse from the throat tubes and the effects of anesthesia, loudly joined in. God, it felt good!

The noise pulled my nurse into the doorway. "Is something wrong?" she asked. We spurted out another round of laughter while the nurse stood grinning at us. Freddie was the first to regain her senses. "I can tell that he's in pain, but he's having trouble explaining it to me." Freddie wouldn't look at me, afraid that she'd lose it again.

With Freddie acting as interpreter, I was finally able to communicate the source of my pain. I could tell from the way she squeezed my hand that she was relieved. Freddie needed everybody, from doctor to nurses to her husband, to get their act together so she could leave for Sedona with some peace of mind. Guilt wouldn't haunt her if she knew my care was on automatic pilot. So it was no surprise that by Saturday Freddie had made giant strides in bringing my pain under better control, convincing the doctor to prescribe my usual fentanyl suckers and instructing the nurses to bring those disgusting treats to me at regular intervals — Freddie knew I wouldn't be smart enough to ask for one until the pain had already escalated.

Comet spent most of her time with Mom and Manny that week, although Freddie took long breaks away from me to walk her and assure her that the hotel was just temporary lodging. But by Saturday morning, Comet's patience was gone. She wanted to see me, and when Freddie opened the SUV's door Comet jumped in and refused to move.

"Out of the car, Comet," Freddie commanded. The greyhound fixed her with the same stony glare she had used during my surgery. Comet got her way.

All intensive care units discourage visitors

other than next of kin and very close friends. "I don't think she can be here," warned the floor nurse when she saw Comet and Freddie approaching the door to my room.

I heard Freddie cheerfully respond, "Oh, she's my husband's service dog."

"Service or not, I don't think animals are allowed in here."

"Why?" Freddie no longer sounded so friendly.

The nurse's softening tone told me that Comet had entered the discussion by simply standing there. "Good question. I don't know. There are people who are allergic to dog hair . . ." The pause in the discussion sounded promising. "If she stays in your husband's room, I can't imagine there would be a problem."

By that time Mom had arrived with Manny in tow. Comet led the group into my room. Until then I had been spinning in and out of reality, wrestling with irksome gaps in memory as I attempted to calculate how much time had elapsed since my surgery. A day? A week? For all I knew it could have been either.

However long it had been, it was too long for Comet. Her fidgeting beside my pillow reminded me of a lovesick teenager who hadn't seen her boyfriend for a *whole day!*

As everybody was settling into the space, the nurse entered and ripped the Velcro on a blood pressure monitor she was removing from a wall bracket. At the sound, Comet's eyes dilated and her rear leg muscles tensed. Freddie saw Comet's alarm. "Comet, don't you —"

A chorus of gasps circled the room as Comet's body shot off the floor. Then, as light as a Colorado snowflake, she landed on the six-inch length of mattress alongside me, not even ruffling the blanket. With a stern glance at the speechless nurse standing on the other side of the bed, Comet settled her lean body onto the narrow landing strip, eyes staring into mine, leaning just enough weight against me to let me know she was there. I was used to Comet's amazing knack of leaping onto a bed without disturbing me in the slightest, but from the openmouthed silence that filled the room, I could tell that the others were suitably impressed. Comet comfortably rested at my side during the remainder of the visit. Freddie finally pried her from the bed with the leash for a late Saturday night departure.

Comet resumed her bed-top vigil on Sunday morning after I was moved out of ICU and into a regular room. By then I was stringing enough words together to form fairly comprehensible sentences. Freddie was surprised at the timing of the room switch, but the doctor told her, "He's tolerating the pain extremely well."

And I was. I didn't want to say anything yet, but I had become increasingly aware of a strange feeling since late Saturday. In spite of the aching and burning in various parts of my sliced and hacked body, I was feeling really good. I didn't want to jump the loading chute by telling anybody else so early on; the narcotics still floating through my abused body might have been inducing a false euphoria. But the pain radiating from the repair efforts was so much less intense than what I had been living with for eight years that I felt as if I had been in nothing more serious than a minor sledding accident.

It soon became apparent that my recovery was proceeding faster than anticipated. As other parts of my body began to catch up to my speech, I was rudely reminded that the three days since surgery was an eon to my intestines. "Freddie, the good news is that I'm finally over most of the effects of the anesthesia." I pulled her down toward the bed so I could whisper into her ear. "The bad news is, I have to go to the bathroom."

"Oh, good!" Freddie exclaimed. "Let me get the bedpan for you!" There are few things in life as obnoxious as the loud voice of a medical professional announcing the prospect of a bowel movement. When that person happens to be your wife broadcasting the news to the rest of the family, it's even more humiliating.

As Mom and Manny scrambled to their feet, I did something really mean. I pushed Comet off the bed. I threw the thin bedsheet away from my body. Then I rolled over. I put my feet on the floor. I pushed myself upright. I was standing — by myself. Without Comet or canes!

"Holy crap!" yelled my mom, never one to hold back on expletives.

Comet pushed her body next to mine, expecting me to lean on her, openly amazed when I did not. I failed to notice that I was swaying like brittle prairie grass in the wind. Freddie rushed through the electric silence to give my weak body some much-needed support. She was clearly stunned. With a dramatic wave of my arm I proclaimed, "To the bathroom, Tonto!"

16

August 2005–October 2006 — Denver and Sedona

Dr. Frey, along with the entire hospital staff, was surprised at how quickly I was able to lift myself off the mattress and onto the floor on that first triumphant trip to the bathroom. But nobody was as shocked as I was. All my life, whenever I had approached an important peak, my health would send me plummeting back down the icy slopes. I would eventually pull myself together and resume the climb to the top, only to topple down and begin all over. Again and again and again . . . Despite my confidence that Dr. Frey could ease some of my pain, by the time I was slapped onto the surgical table, my expectations had been pathetically low. *Just let me have one hour — one measly period of sixty minutes — where I feel any-where as good as I used to. Just give me a* memory *of what feeling good was like.*

During the first week after surgery, I attributed the twenty minutes that would elapse between stabs of leg pain to anesthesia and all the other drugs swimming through my system. When my feet didn't burn as if someone were scorching them with a cigar lighter, I didn't allow myself to believe the pain could actually have diminished. When I stood up from bed, accepting Freddie's help to the bathroom, I was scared to give voice to the nagging notion that I felt pretty damn good considering what I'd been through. *If it seems too good to be true, it is. Don't even think it. You'll just be crushed tomorrow.*

At three o'clock in the morning, six days after surgery, I was on my feet and walking the halls hands-free for the first time in eight years — no canes, no walker, and no dog — weeks earlier than anybody had anticipated. Every incredible step down that long corridor caused a fresh round of gleeful sobbing, although I tried to stifle my tears, not wanting to tempt fate. *Could it be? Can this actually be happening to me?* "Yes, yes, YES! Oh God, YES!" Until I started shouting, the floor nurses hadn't even recognized me. My detour into the shower room caused an alert for "patient needing assistance," but the nurse's presence in the bathroom didn't dent my spirits as I stood there joyously, water pouring over my stitched and swollen body.

Freddie and Comet departed for Sedona early on Tuesday morning, planning to return to Denver in a week. Comet had to be physically removed from my bed, Freddie dragging her dead weight down the hallway while I listened to her nails scrape on the tile floor. Before she left, Freddie warned me, "Just take your time." But not even her suspicions could dampen my determination to get out of the hospital as fast as I could.

Dr. Frey's office had not anticipated making physical therapy arrangements outside the hospital for another two weeks, but I skated through in-patient therapy in two swift sessions, so hospital protocol and insurance dictated that I be placed in an off-site setting for the duration of my recovery. I called Freddie to report my miraculous progress.

"So I'm out of here on Friday," I crowed.

"*What?* You can't be serious," my wife sputtered. "Why can't you ever do things the normal way? You . . . you . . ."

Ignoring Freddie's not-so-ambiguous response, I continued with my scheme to escape the hospital. Before she had time to plan her return, I was transported to a room in the long-term assisted living facility that had been designated as my rehab center. I lasted all of two days before calling a taxi. It wasn't that the rehab people weren't good at their jobs; it's just that I didn't want to stick around after the first Code Blue resulted in a sheet-covered gurney being wheeled past my room. And I can't lie: the thought of giving myself the remainder of my required blood-thinning injections while enjoying a room-service rib eye and soft plush sheets appealed to me. I don't think it helped Freddie's state of mind when I told her I would be waiting for her at a hotel. She knew me too well.

Freddie's frosty mood during her three-day Colorado "vacation" — staying in the hotel while we completed my blood-thinning regimen — signaled that she questioned my sanity. Dr. Frey, though, believed my promises that I wouldn't do anything foolish if he released me many weeks earlier than originally planned. He was reassured by the fact that Freddie had medical experience.

"I'm back!" was my unofficial mantra on the drive from Denver to Sedona. Comet's shining eyes and adoring stares told me that she liked my mood. Freddie did not share Comet's enthusiasm.

"Why do you always have to prove that you're meaner and tougher, that you can do twice what the doctors order? Why don't you feel like you deserve the luxury of taking your time? I'm telling you now, do not rush this rehab and then say you did it to make my life easier. *Je te connais.* Don't do it."

Ultimately, however, my buoyant attitude was contagious. Even cautious Freddie caught the bug. I was walking again, and the truth was that my entire family desperately wanted the same result I did. Sandoz seemed both befuddled and overjoyed at the new me. Once we were back in Sedona, I launched into a regimen of physical therapy that included at-home exercises and sessions at a facility in Sedona. A blissful smile never left my face as I sampled the freedoms of walking on a treadmill or peddling a stationary bike. Comet was treated as a favored guest and provided with her own exercise mat on which to rest as she monitored my efforts. She seemed to be energized by the people who were helping me, going out of her way to greet the therapists. She had never before shown any inclination to express affection to strangers (unless they were uniformed).

With the passing of each muscle-strengthening day, it became easier for me to believe that I was cured. On the surface I certainly seemed to be a different man. One of our neighbors, a kindly retiree named Madeleine, had been watching me stumble around ever since I moved to Sedona. We shared a fondness for books and I would often discuss them with her when she was in her yard. About three weeks after my return, I ventured out of the house for a walk around the block. Comet assisted with my balance, but I was not bent over my canes. Madeleine was the first person we ran into. She approached us and then stopped, squinting up at my face with a puzzled expression.

"Hi, Madeleine."

"You must be Wolf's brother," she finally decided. "You sound like him, too, but you're a little taller." It was the first time in five years that any of my neighbors had seen me standing upright.

"Madeleine, it's me. Wolf."

Her lips pursed. After examining my face for several more moments, she murmured, "Yeah, okay, I'll take your word for it," and continued down the street, plainly unconvinced.

I encountered similar incredulous reactions from the fraternity of people who had entered my orbit during my Sedona years. The first time Bill and Jana spied me walking alone, I thought somebody had just told them they had won the lottery. Rindy's embrace when I stopped by her real estate office almost sent me back to Denver. Pam, whom I had avoided for almost a year as I became increasingly hopeless about my health, cried with happiness. Ben couldn't hug me enough. Not one of these friends recognized me at first. It always took a double or triple take for them to be sure it was me. People started sticking around for celebratory dinners that covered all hours of the night. The misidentifications, astonished reactions, and subsequent compliments about my upright posture and healthy glow were like cotton candy to a kid. The buzzing high kept me revved up far more than was good for me.

The increased speed of the world I now lived in just served as a reminder of how much time I had lost, creating a manic circle — having more made me want more. Even though I was often exhausted, my muscles knotted from unfamiliar levels of activity, I considered those feelings to be a reward for hard work, sort of like the feeling that used to overtake me during football practices in college. By the end of September, I con-

315

vinced Freddie that I was strong enough to fly by myself (without Comet) to Omaha to surprise Kylie at the ceremony for her admission to the Nebraska State Bar Association. It was my first solo flight in eight years. Kylie and Lindsey were dumbstruck by my appearance and good cheer.

"Dad, I hardly recognized you! You look so . . . so . . . healthy!" Kylie had a lot on her plate that day, but her tears were for me. Lindsey's eyes were moist, too, but her response was more reserved. "You look great, Dad, but how are you feeling?"

"Like a million bucks!"

"Really?"

"Linds, this is the real thing. Dr. Frey is a miracle worker."

"If you say so."

I let her skeptical tone ride, preferring to assume that, like Freddie, my daughters now believed in this fairy tale. The frog was once again a prince!

Judges, lawyers, and clerks who attended the swearing-in ceremony went out of their way to find me and marvel at my transformation. "I can't believe it's you! You look so good! I would never have recognized you!" Little did they know that their comments were fueling my unspoken desire to return to practicing law. After all, at age fifty-one I should be at the peak of my profession.

I ignored the first inklings that it might be wise to take my expectations down a few notches. After flying to Omaha, driving another hour to the state's Capitol Building in Lincoln, attending the ceremony and joining in several celebrations that followed, I was unable to sleep. That night my pelvis began to throb uncontrollably, almost in rhythm to the stabbing of my feet and toes. "Just inflamed nerves. It's going to take a while for everything to calm down. It doesn't happen overnight," I mumbled to myself, prayerlike, while I massaged my feet. Three days of bed rest after my return to Sedona, and I was back — again!

Comet was in the midst of her own adjustments. She had known me when she was simply a pet whom I thoroughly enjoyed as a companion and roommate. She had no expectations of me beyond trusting that I would walk her, be kind to her, and make sure the food in her bowl didn't get stale. Comet then became one of my primary caretakers, a relationship that imposed enormous duties on her and transformed her role from friend to supervisor. As a service dog, Comet expected me to act less like a drinking buddy and more like a mature adult who cared about his own safety. For the past four years I had depended on her every moment that I was not in a chair or a bed.

Now, however, I no longer required Comet to help me balance when I got out of bed. I could usually wrangle myself out of a chair without her assistance, and I could walk around the house unaided by dog or cane. Comet the service dog wasn't needed as often. Then again, I occasionally still asked her to pull me to my feet or help me balance. Comet had a hard time figuring out what her role was supposed to be. Sometimes when I was upright and unassisted she would look utterly confused, her tail pulled up under her abdomen and her eyes pinched and worried.

"Would you quit it? We've talked about this! Get out of the way!" After my return from Omaha I had been confident that I could walk around outdoors without dog or canes. Comet wasn't buying it, and had begun bracing herself across the front doorway, refusing to budge and blocking me whenever I tried to exit.

"I already told you. I do not need a crutch!" Squeezing my body past the rigid dog, I would depart. Comet would scrunch through the narrow opening before I could slam the door shut. I'm positive that the only reason she wanted to come along was so that she could revel in the exquisite "I told you so" moment that was usually only fifteen minutes away.

"Don't tell me I have to walk all the way back to the front door to get a cane." Leaning on Comet, I would stumble back, muttering to her all the way, "Don't act so cocky. I might just hook you up to the walker."

As long as I remembered cane and dog, I was soon able to negotiate my way around our oversized lot — for the very first time. My stroll around every vivid square foot of trees, shrubs, and flowering sage and cactus felt like a visit to a world-class botanical garden. As my mood improved, I went from admiring the landscaping to pruning, trimming, and irrigating. I had some understanding of the physical changes that were making my muscles sore and tired as they were increasingly challenged, but I also chose this period, over my doctor's strong objections, to try to eliminate all my pain medications so I could determine my baseline of discomfort.

As I dialed back the medications over the passing weeks, withdrawal symptoms stressed my already fragile systems. I was enormously fatigued from simple exercises that I hadn't done by myself in years, such as walking, although admittedly the walks now covered far more distance than they should have. As my body cleansed itself, I started detecting throbbing and burning that I prayed was just temporary phantom pain.

"Don't you think you should spend a little less time gardening and more time getting some healthy rest?" This was Freddie's daily refrain, eventually becoming more of a rote comment than a statement of concern as winter and spring passed into the summer of 2006. Freddie would return home from work to find me splayed on a chaise lounge, nearly comatose from the day's efforts. At least I had the sense to situate myself on the shady patio and have a gin and tonic waiting for her. But she wasn't interested. "I was hoping we could meet some friends at the Village Pub. There's a jazz group playing tonight. But I guess you're too tired. Again."

Kylie and Lindsey often called me in the early evening when they got out of classes or were done working for the day. Increasingly, however, Freddie had to tell them that I had fallen into bed at five o'clock. She would assure the girls that my recovery was progressing, but they were dubious. So was

Jackie. The third time she visited from Flagstaff specifically to see me, only to find me oblivious to her presence, she told her mom, "From now on I'll just call."

The stress of trying to produce a perfect recovery caused me to revert to bad habits. Instead of the half hour of daily therapeutic exercises prescribed by my physical therapist, I did two one-hour sessions every day. Walking became my own personal marathon. Pruning now included raking and lifting. Not even old clients were safe. My phone bill ballooned as I began setting the stage for my return to law. Because my mind had become as flexible as a steel post by the time my wife moved to Arizona, Freddie had been forced into the role of bookkeeper. She continued in that role primarily because we both still had doubts about my ability to deal with details. I was great on my big picture expectations, but the little things? Not so good. I waited for her to question the phone charges, but she said nothing.

One morning, as I was trimming some overgrown sage bushes, I noticed smears of blood on the patio. I followed the trail back out over the rough red granite chunks that were spread over the backyard and then thought to look at the soles of my feet. They were cut up and bleeding from walking barefoot on the rock cover. I put on some shoes and kept working, ignoring the fact that my feet apparently had no feeling.

I should have known something was up when my retorts to Freddie that "I don't need to rest" started being met with a monotone, "Fine. I'm too tired to argue." When I tried to tell my girls about my impressive recovery and they cut me off with, "Please, Dad, can we not talk about it?" it should have slapped me out of the fairy tale. When Freddie drove the entire way to Denver for my one-year checkup while I slumped in the passenger's seat, I still didn't get it. I wasn't recovering. I was more like an overtrained quarterhorse, fit on the surface but dangerously fatigued and heading for a crippling fall.

The visit with Dr. Frey started out swimmingly. "This x-ray looks wonderful. See all the white along here?" His pen pointed along boxy white outlines and distinct screw shapes that constituted what now served as my spine. "This is new bone being formed in your disc spaces and along the outside of the vertebrae. It looks like it's all filling in solidly. Barring anything crazy, you should have a good solid fusion along that whole area."

The good news gave me goose bumps.

"That's great! When do you think I'll be able to return to work?" There was no point in wasting any more of the doctor's time.

Dr. Frey's smile faded, replaced with a pensive look as he took a seat on the wheeled stool. He didn't believe in wasting time either. "You're not going to be returning to work. You're not cured. We've just made your condition tolerable."

"What the hell are you talking about? I've read plenty of stories on the Internet about people who go right back to their normal lives after these surgeries." I didn't care if there hadn't been enough surgeries like mine to make that type of anecdotal evidence relevant.

"It's true that we sometimes release patients without restrictions once all of the bone grows in. We don't like to set ceilings on what they can or can't do. But your pain symptoms are still in the upper range, even after a year. I want you continuing to do whatever you can within reason, but I also want you to remember how bad you felt before the surgery. If I told you to go back to snow skiing or golf, would you?"

"Probably."

"Then you haven't learned a thing. I'm afraid that a lot of your pain is chronic and will always limit you. I'm also confident that if you went right back to doing those types of things, whatever is causing your discs to degenerate would move up to the healthy part of your spine. Besides, you're a long way from even being able to sit unassisted on the floor. Your rehab has been great, but you're trying to overcome decades of damage."

It was time to stop pouting and start negotiating. "Okay. I'll come back in six months and we can talk about it then."

Dr. Frey smiled. "I'll be glad to revisit the issue anytime you want. But let me ask you something. Isn't one miracle enough for you? Why don't you find something more useful to do than pestering people with lawsuits?" The doctor laughed at his own joke. I don't care how intelligent he was, I was downright hilarious next to this guy.

I left the doctor's office deeply shaken by Dr. Frey's final pronouncement: "I don't think you'll ever go back to your old profession. Just staying healthy enough to walk unaided will be your full-time job from now on." It didn't dawn on me for at least ten minutes that Freddie hadn't spoken a word since we got into the car. Now I watched her intently studying traffic that was backed up on I-25 before our exit to the hotel. "Hey, it's not as bad as it sounds," I insisted.

"In six more months he'll think twice about that miracle comment."

But the harder I tried to get our life back to the way it was, the more irritable Freddie became. I knew all was not Sedona rosy red in our house, but I was too frustrated and angry to do anything about it. As I read it, Freddie was clearly unhappy that her prince was never going to present her with a glass slipper. So be it. I stuffed what I perceived to be her disappointment in the same mental folder as my daughters' apparent lack of interest in my recovery. If I could just concentrate long enough, work hard enough, keep nose to grindstone, they'd all come around.

17

March–October 2006 — Sedona and Omaha
It was a sunny March day, crisp with the possibilities of spring. As had become her new routine, Freddie sprinted past my spot on the patio when she got home. I could see her sitting in the living room, waiting to talk with me. What she had to say did not take long.

"I'm leaving you."

"Knock it off. I'm too tired to think that's funny."

"I'm not making a joke. I'm leaving you — tonight." Her words were not frantic or loud, but as matter-of-fact as if she had been planning to leave for some time. Which she had.

"Come on, Freddie. Stop it. What'd I do to piss you off this time?" We had been having our share of arguments lately.

"This time? *This time!* Why do you always think our arguments are my fault? That I'm always pissed off at something?" Freddie turned to a small suitcase that was already packed and waiting in the entryway. "It's time for me to go."

My mouth was open far enough to dislocate my jaw. I was stunned at the look of resolve on Freddie's face as she wheeled the suitcase out the door.

"Wait a minute! What's going on? You can't be serious!"

"Steve, listen to me. Don't get mad, just listen. I can't stand our life any longer. I can't stand coming home to an obsessive crazy person who just can't get on with life."

"Freddie! We need to talk. You haven't said a word to me about any of this. You can't just walk out on me without talking about it!"

"Oh, Steve. I *have* tried to talk to you. Your only response to how I feel is, 'Hang in there.' I don't want to hang in there anymore. There's no light at the end of the cave . . . or whatever. I am leaving you." Freddie was standing straight, tapping courage in a way that would have been heroic in other circumstances.

"You're only leaving me because I haven't been able to return us to our past life of luxury. Admit it!"

"Yes, that's exactly why I'm leaving,"

Freddie said quietly, and then, "I wouldn't care if the only thing you could ever do was pick up people's garbage or nothing at all. But if *you* don't return us to our past life, *you'll* feel so guilty and be so mad at yourself for 'failing' that it'll be almost like the surgery never happened. You've been trying so hard to prove you can overcome everything that you don't have anything left, for me or anyone else. I can't live like that anymore."

She pulled her suitcase to the car, shoved it inside, and drove away. The entire conversation had taken less than ten minutes.

For the next three weeks I could hardly function. Anger drove me from room to room or out back to furiously rip and hack at the trees and shrubs. All I could focus on was "I was wronged!" Every bit of my energy had been devoted to recovering and getting our past life back. I wanted our family to be strong again. It was all up to me! I was pushing myself past exhaustion to prove to Freddie that I was the man she had married. I wanted to be in shape, run for miles, have a body fat of 8 percent, bicycle a hundred miles a weekend. I wanted to be all that I once was. Freddie just didn't get it! How could I "get on with life" being only a small fraction of the person I could have

328

been? Should have been?

Comet suffered Freddie's absence in an entirely different way. Even more than most dogs, greyhounds thrive on routine, and Comet's was now severely altered. Instead of greeting Freddie after the workday, being fed within an hour after that, and seducing Freddie into giving her three treats — always and only three — Comet now began her evening by stretching onto the rug in the foyer. She would stare at the front door, ears perking at the slightest outside sound, refusing to relax until it was dark. Yet she didn't seem angry that she had been slighted. Her expressions and body language told me she was more concerned than ir-ritated. *Why are you mad at me? I will tell you I'm sorry. What did I do wrong? I'll correct it. When are you coming home? I still love you.*

I heard through back channels that Freddie had moved in with a girlfriend. Meanwhile, Freddie steadfastly refused to permit any of our friends to give me her new address or even a phone number. By early summer my manic yard work, sessions of exercise, and miles of walking slowed and then stopped. Instead, I sat in my chaise lounge outside until the heat became too intense, then moved indoors to sink deeper into my personal assessment: one failed marriage and possibly a second, daughters who were emotionally wrung out, pain that persisted regardless of how hard I rehabbed or how much I exercised, and the reality of permanent disability and unemployment.

Lying in my recliner with Comet curled at my feet, I drifted back to the black-and-white Westerns I had watched as a kid. The plots were always the same. Man rolls into town, man meets girl, outlaws rob bank, man gets shot. Then man captures outlaws! He saves the bank, gets the girl, she nurses him back to health, and he rides into the sunset alone so he can do it all again the next week. There was never a time when the cowboy sat down in the middle of the road and moaned about life's unfairness.

The community where I grew up was not unlike one of those dusty towns, and the lessons I learned around the dinner table echoed the same themes. My father earned the respect and devotion of his family by staunchly following that code of conduct. Being a man meant something. Women weren't weak in Dad's family, but it was unforgivable if the men around them weren't capable of providing primary protection and sustenance. Dad was sixteen years old when he left the family farm, twenty when he married my sixteen-year-old mother, and twenty-three when he secured himself a "city job" so he could support his wife and two children. When he said, "It's a man's job to take care of his own family, no matter what. Don't complain. Don't make excuses. Just do it," I didn't question him.

As the only male in our immediate family, I was expected to fill the leadership role when my father died. But by 1997 my health was already tempering those expectations. After Dad passed away, I was not able to step up and take over. Instead, I was sliding into disability, dependent on my wife, unable to work hard enough to overcome my pain. All I could focus on was my failure to tough it out and live up to the code.

In the long days alone with Comet and Sandoz, it now occurred to me that if my father were alive he might have a few things to say about the situation I currently found myself in. He might have given me a hard shake and demanded, "What the hell is wrong with you? You have three daughters and a wife who need you. You can't be there for them if you're hiding in the house like a little kid who had his feelings hurt at school. Act like a man. Buck up and get your ass out of that chair. Stop feeling sorry for yourself."

Losing all perspective while I obsessed about my "failures" was detestable, but voluntarily surrendering marriage and family because of pride was a sin. The coping strategies I had relied on all my life — denial, isolation, stubbornness, silence — now revealed themselves to be as useless as rusty old farm tools. When had strength curdled into self-sabotage? I couldn't put a finger on it. But in the middle of the afternoon, I clearly heard my dad saying, *Family is the most important thing.*

"I know," I agreed out loud.

The living room blared a barbed silence back at me.

A man's humblest hour is when he compares his life story as it is with what he had hoped to make it. I was not only humbled, I was embarrassed. Freddie's parting words to me — "I need to be away from you" — were harsh, and they left little room for interpretation. But my daughters hadn't given up on me. I could start the next chapter of my story with them.

I was reminded of the old days as I prepared for my trip. Food needed to be trashed, mail had to be canceled, and Sandoz had to be situated at the neighbors'. Since, as always, Comet would be my traveling companion and copilot, there would need to be plenty of her favorite food and treats on board, as well as a stuffed animal or two. I told enough people who circulated around Sedona that I was traveling to Nebraska so that word could filter to Freddie, allowing her to remove the rest of her belongings from the house while I was gone.

It was time to heal the important parts of my life; my body could wait. But I was scared. What if I didn't approach the girls just right? Neither Kylie nor Lindsey knew I was coming for a visit. After spinning in a world of uncertainty during the drive, I decided to fall back on a tried-and-true rule: When in doubt, do anything, but do it today. An hour outside of Omaha I called Kylie and told her, "I don't know how long I'll be in town, so I'd like to have dinner with you and Lindsey this weekend."

Kylie's response was wary. "Well, I'll try to get in touch with Lindsey and see what her plans are. Let's shoot for Friday evening."

When Freddie left me I had called Kylie and Lindsey and told them the news. Freddie had kept in touch with the girls but had not confided in them. Friday night, as we sat down for dinner at one of our favorite restaurants, they couldn't wait to vent their anger at the absent party.

"I'm really mad at Freddie," Lindsey announced. "I don't know what she's thinking or doing, but it feels like she left the whole family. And didn't that girlfriend she's living with leave her husband last year? Sounds like Freddie's having a midlife crisis."

"I agree with Lindsey. Freddie's acting like she's gone wacko," Kylie chimed in.

"Don't be too hard on her, girls. She has her reasons." Being the oldest adult, it was my duty to impose a sense of decorum. Besides, I was increasingly convinced that Freddie had been justified in leaving, even though I missed her terribly. I took a deep breath.

"Look, I think everyone sitting here can agree about one thing. I have what I guess you could call a personality glitch." The daughters froze and stared at me. "I've always felt like I had to show strength at all times, to all people, even in the slightest crisis. I think that's been hard for Freddie to live with. And maybe for you."

"But you were sick," Kylie objected.

"Doesn't matter. We're a family. What was happening with me affected everyone, but I wouldn't let anyone else have an opinion about it. Especially over the past year."

Kylie and Lindsey exchanged perplexed glances and let the topic drop. I was practically hyperventilating from this confession, but I don't think they noticed.

Over the next ten days of my stay Kylie and Lindsey kept criticizing Freddie, but I knew part of their anger was misdirected. They also had plenty of pent-up hostility toward me. The girls had been in their teens and early twenties when my illness struck. They didn't have the experience to comprehend my depression and withdrawal from the family. My manic behavior after the surgery had to have been just as disturbing. I could have promised them, "I've changed," but instead I vowed to myself that I would prove it.

I left Omaha feeling better about my prospects as a father. Rebuilding my reputation with my daughters was a worthy goal, even if it had to be done in increments of weekly phone calls and the occasional visit. I had the time, and for once I also had the patience. I had learned from watching Comet that you could gracefully leave an old you behind, concentrating on each day's offerings and knowing that there might be purposes in life quite different from the ones you had originally chosen. It wasn't failure. It was life. If I had not learned these lessons in time to preserve my marriage, it wasn't too late for me to show my daughters that I was a father they could once again depend on.

Back home in Sedona, I grew physically stronger by the day. I still had trouble socializing in groups of more than a few people, but my mind was clearing. I accepted that certain amounts of pain medication would always be a part of my life. As long as I took advantage of a flexible schedule to rest and properly medicate, the pain was no longer totally debilitating. It was obvious that no one was going to hire me to practice law, because I couldn't guarantee that I could string enough consecutive hours together to be a productive employee. As far I was concerned, sitting in a straight chair or standing up for more than twenty minutes at a time was a feat best left to the young and able.

But there were some new things that I wanted to explore. I had always loved to read, both for the distraction and for the solace. Literature offered perspective on my personal trials and had pulled me through some very long nights. I had been devouring mysteries since I was a boy, and during all but my most painful days, they still had the power to captivate me. I spent enough time with them that I had begun to fantasize about writing one myself. The Native American Rights Foundation newsletter, which I received every month, was full of fascinating legal cases that could be an ideal jumping-off point for a mystery series. Why not? I needed something to keep myself busy. Golf and snow skiing were certainly out of the question.

18

November 2006–December 2010 — New Mexico, Arizona, Nebraska

Comet and I had been alone for nine months when I decided to travel to Albuquerque, New Mexico, for the Tony Hillerman Writers Conference. I had learned of this annual seminar for aspiring writers from a magazine announcement. Initially I scoffed at the idea of attending. Although I was sharper than I had been prior to surgery, it was still hard for me to absorb information quickly. Worse, I had zero technical knowledge about writing or publishing outside of the narrow parameters of the law. That meant I would be voluntarily exposing my fragile ego to potential embarrassment. I rationalized taking that risk by telling myself that if I liked the hotel that was the site of the conference, it could be a convenient future resting place when I trekked from Sedona to Omaha. Besides,

Comet would enjoy the vacation.

Thanks to our many road trips, Comet was now a discriminating traveler. Over time she had become a "resort dog," accustomed to the finer things in life, such as attention from hotel guests and leftovers from room service. My one indulgence on the Nebraska-Arizona trail was a stop at an upscale hotel in the Denver Tech Center, fifteen minutes from the spine institute. Once Comet had experienced the impressive thread counts of the hotel's sheets, a phone that could summon treats on a whim, and the "beautiful people" who were often in attendance, she scrutinized the standard roadside motel with the attitude of a supermodel: *No way.* Whenever I steered into a parking lot that lacked a grand entryway and a valet, Comet's eyes would widen in panic in my rearview mirror. She would refuse to jump out of the vehicle and I would have to drag her by the leash from the back of the SUV.

Comet enthusiastically approved of my decision to attend the Albuquerque conference. When we made our appearance in the hotel lobby, the staff at the front desk spent a good five minutes fawning over her — proof that they had superior taste. The faculty and students reacted to Comet with smiles, sighs, and gushing acknowledgment of her royalty, reinforcing her opinion that we were in the presence of the right kind of people. The crowning moment of the week, however, was Comet's introduction to Tony Hillerman.

It was the end of the four-day conference, and I was tired. Not only was I receiving a crash education about the world of writing, I had been sitting in an upright chair for extended periods — an hour or longer — for the first time in at least six years. I occasionally got up and took a brief walk to relieve the pressure on my spine, but for the most part I was upright on my butt. My abdomen and sides had begun to ache as if I had absorbed twelve rounds of body punches from Muhammad Ali. Now Comet and I stood waiting for the elevator to take us to the final function, that night's awards banquet. Exercising her impeccable manners, Comet waited for disembarking passengers before she led the way through the open elevator doors.

"Hi, Wolf." Anne Hillerman, a tall, energetic woman who sparkled with warm enthusiasm and a gorgeous smile, was already in the elevator. She had befriended me during the course of the conference, introducing me to aspiring writers, published authors, and faculty members. I yanked on Comet's leash when I saw the other person in the elevator, suddenly at a loss for words.

"How are you two tonight?" Anne was asking. When I just grinned, she continued, "Wolf, this is my dad, Tony."

Mr. Hillerman stuck his hand out in greeting. "Glad to meet you, Wolf." He smiled down at Comet. "And who is this?"

I finally replied, "It's a pleasure to meet you, Mr. Hillerman. Comet, you can say hi."

Before I could tell him that he was one of my favorite authors, he observed, "Must be a female, she's smaller than a typical male. Greyhounds. Did you know . . ." For the next two minutes of the elevator ride and the five minutes more that it took to walk to the banquet hall, he casually recited an encyclopedic primer on the greyhound breed that left me wondering if, in addition to talent, he possessed a photographic memory.

I had intentionally arrived early in order to reserve a seat at a table that kept Comet out of traffic and allowed me room to move around when I could no longer sit. Despite the euphoria of meeting a man whose work I had enjoyed for decades, I hadn't been sitting for more than ten minutes when my ribs began to throb. Suddenly a prick of burning flared in a spot about halfway up my spine, a sensation I hadn't felt since before my surgery. Past episodes had taught me that something serious was about to happen if this brush fire wasn't extinguished right away. I pulled Comet to her feet and we hurried to the elevator.

By the time I entered my room ten minutes later, every attempt to suck air into my lungs made a wheezing sound. My jaw was aching and my clothing was soaked. I stripped everything off, throwing my pants and shirt on the floor as I stumbled to the thermostat. I dialed it to the lowest setting and then aimed for the bed. As I hit the mattress, a searing pain stabbed an area below my sternum. Black spots crowded my vision and I reached for the phone, jabbing at the button for the front desk. "I'm sick. I need help," I croaked.

Five minutes later a hollow pounding sounded from the door and a man's voice called, "Mr. Wolf. Mr. Wolf, are you okay? We're having trouble with the lock. The card reader's not working. Mr. Wolf?"

Trouble with the lock? This is a four-star hotel, for crying out loud! My fingernails dug into my palms as I silently raged at my stupidity. How could I have ignored the familiar signs — the aching muscles and stabbing pain that circled my ribs? I slammed my fists into the bed and tried to yell out, but the weak thuds, accompanied by my soft whimper, merely melted into the scuffling sounds and rising voices of the people on the other side of the door. Through parched lips I finally slurred, "Hold on. I'll get the door open."

"What?"

I could hear plans being made to force the door open from the hallway. The electronic lock had given me some problems the previous day, but it had been repaired. *It worked for me,* I thought desperately, already slipping into unconsciousness. Comet had leaped onto the bed and was resting her head on my chest, staring at me intently. Her ears pointed upward in question marks of concern.

"Comet, get the door," I gasped.

Thank God the handle was a lever and not a knob. Comet glanced at me and flew off the bed, somehow maintaining her greyhound dignity during her rush to the door. She reached a paw up and pulled down hard on the handle. It clicked open and Comet backed away as two medics dashed into the room, firing urgent questions.

Whenever the burn in my back got bad enough, arteries in my heart would spasm, restricting the blood flow — a heart attack without a blood clot. I whispered a quick summary of this condition and the medics instantly placed a tab of nitroglycerin under my tongue. Within minutes the arteries began to open, allowing me to finally inhale the oxygen flowing through the tube in my nose. My heart rhythms were already stabilizing by the time I was lifted onto a gurney for transportation to a local hospital. Since I was newborn-naked, the medics wrapped me in blankets. There was a frantic discussion about "What do we do with the dog?" but it became abundantly clear from Comet's tense stance and unsmiling eyes that she was coming with me.

"She's my service dog and we're here alone. Besides, she's the one who opened the door for you." A medic nodded and Comet trotted alongside my gurney as we rolled into the hall. By the time I was wheeled through the hotel lobby (packed with gaping guests) and settled into the ambulance, the rescue squad was already referring to Comet as "sweetie" and assuring her, "Don't worry, he'll be okay." For her brave part in the rescue, Comet was allowed to ride in the front of the ambulance, keeping a close eye on the medics as they hovered over me in the back.

Comet stayed by my side after we were deposited in the emergency room, where the doctor decided that I had not had a "traditional" heart attack and my vital signs were approaching normal. Still, he wanted more tests. The rest of the staff had other concerns. "What do we do with Comet?" It had only taken five minutes for her name to filter throughout the ER. The question came from one of several techs who had gathered near my room, and it instantly set off a spirited competition about who would be primary custodian.

An hour later I returned to a small room where Comet lay on a pile of sheets and blankets that had been plumped on the floor for her. By 4:00 a.m. the doctor gave me a thumbs-up. "The nitro was administered just in time. It doesn't appear that you suffered any heart damage, but I wouldn't advise traveling without nitro close at hand." He told the attending nurse that I could be released later in the morning if I didn't suffer any relapses.

After the medical staff had deserted my room, I lay in the semidarkness listening to the silence and the occasional squeak of a nurse's shoes on the linoleum floor. I looked at Comet. She gazed at me steadily from her nest of snowy bedding. In the stillness of the hospital room, I couldn't avoid the unhappy truth. There was only one reason I was here alone: *me.* My visit with the girls had begun to convince them that I was no longer in furious denial about my physical limitations. I was sure they wanted their dad back and that I could eventually rebuild those bonds. Now it was time to make amends to the one person who had unstintingly supported me in sickness and in health. I truly would be a failure if I didn't at least try to honor the "until death do we part" portion of those vows.

"Comet, we need to go back to Sedona and talk to Freddie." Comet's head shot up. I swear she was smiling.

Freddie had relented and given me her phone number a few weeks earlier, and I had apologized for my obsessive focus on failure, weakness, and all the creaky codes of valor that had skewed my behavior throughout our marriage and later prevented me from appreciating my new lease on life. But my apologies seemed so trivial in light of all that had happened. I had to show Freddie that the stranger who had kidnapped her husband eight years ago was now nothing more than a pile of compost. There was one small ray of hope: before I left for New Mexico, Freddie had asked, "Do you think Comet would like to spend a day with me? I miss her. Maybe you can drop her off."

What a man can accomplish with just an address! Freddie had tried to ignore me the first time we met more than nineteen years ago, but I had been determined to get her attention. She had told me she worked in cardiology, so I fell to the floor from a bar stool and faked a heart attack (oh, the irony). A subtler but no less spectacular approach might be needed this time. I called a florist in Sedona and had twelve dozen roses (yes, 144) delivered to her door. Why twelve dozen? That's all the florist could get her hands on. The next arrangement a few days later, with seventy-five tall tropical blooms, was fewer in quantity but far more impressive in size. I knew that Freddie was too intelligent to fall for something so obvious, but I wanted her to know that my thoughts about her were at least as grand as the flower arrangements. Freddie's thoughts about me, however, were quite different.

Although Freddie had phoned to thank me for the flowers, her subsequent calls and emails were not as kind. She refused to meet with me in person. During several long conversations, she explained why. Even in the darkest of times over those past trying years, she said, she had always maintained a glimmer of optimism. The hope that something good would eventually emerge made the trudge a tolerable adventure. When, after my surgery, I reverted to obsessive, ill-advised rehab, Freddie became convinced that the worst part of my personality was now what would permanently define me — and finally kill the most vital part of her. "I can't live a life without some kind of promise, some chance of laughing and good times," she said. It all made sense to me. I didn't tell Freddie, but for my part, I missed the high-spirited bon vivant I had fallen in love with. Freddie's essence had been smothered to the brink of extinction not by her duties as nurse and breadwinner but by my relentless determination to get to some version of perfect.

On a day that dawned with a frigid voice message reminding me to take Sandoz to the vet, I called Freddie to share my insights about our relationship. "But talking about it over the phone is so impersonal," I added. "We should get together for dinner." She wasn't buying what I was selling.

"Steve, listen to me. I miss our house and the dogs. I miss our daughters desperately. Kylie and Lindsey won't even talk to me. I even miss you a little." Freddie paused. I heard her take a deep breath. "But I don't know if I could live with you again."

Her words cored into my heart like an auger. "Freddie, how can you mean that? You can't throw seventeen years of marriage and a wonderful family away. You just can't." My last statement was forced out in a whisper.

"Why not? You did."

My repeated calls to her throughout that week and the next ended the same way, if she answered at all.

But did I get discouraged? Come on! After Freddie realized I had faked my heart attack that first night we met, she had told the bouncer to commit severe bodily harm if I approached her table to talk. I had given him three hundred dollars to ignore Freddie's orders. It was the best money I ever spent. My persistence this time, however, could not be expressed with stunts more befitting a teenager. We were long past the golden retriever stage — *Do you love me? Do you, do you, do you?* I preferred the greyhound approach, best summed up by the saying, "Life is not about waiting for the storms to pass; it's about learning to dance in the rain." I wanted Freddie to know that I finally grasped that concept. If I was extremely lucky, it would mean something to her.

I sent Freddie a bouquet of deep pink roses and lilies and called her again. "There's a great jazz band playing at the Pub. How about dinner and music?"

Freddie didn't hang up. She even chuckled. "You don't give up, do you? Thanks for the flowers. But I thought I told you I need some space."

"You did? My short-term memory is still shaky."

"No."

"Yes. The doctor said I'm like a trauma victim. Regaining memory skills will take a while longer."

"No. I meant no to a date."

"No?"

"Yes."

"Good. I'll pick you up at seven."

Freddie laughed out, "I give up," before she disconnected.

A series of "I'm not dating you" dates followed, all allowing Freddie to finally express her greatest fear about having any future relationship with me. It kept coming back to trust.

"How do I know that what you're saying will last? How do I know that the first time you find out that you can't meet your own expectations, you won't revert right back to Mr. Lone Cowboy? I can't go through that again. I know that your spine is better, but it won't always be about your back."

"You don't know. And my promising that I won't go 'Lone Cowboy' has about as much value as a time-share in Guantánamo. I'm just now figuring out what happened. It's amazing how my mind fell apart as fast as my body."

Freddie gave me a long look and nodded her head slightly. She allowed herself a small smile, which suddenly widened into a grin. "I've been waiting for you to start spinning your fantasies about the future. You haven't. Not once during all of our talks. You even tried to dance with me last week. You remind me of the good old days." Freddie raised her wineglass. "Santé."

That cheer to my health didn't cure everything, but it did signal a new direction. The dates that followed weren't always placid, but neither of us ever left the table feeling guilty or cheated. The only time the past was discussed was in the context of trying to make things better. No blame, just a mutual agreement that it wasn't worth

351

another visit. We also agreed to quit spending so much time worrying about tomorrow. We had seen firsthand how little control
we had over it. By the time I prepared a
Thanksgiving meal, complete with a
champagne-basted turkey and all the trim-
mings, we were talking about how to get
Freddie's belongings back into the house.
"Just don't get used to me cooking," I
cautioned. "Neither of us wants that."

My recovery was long and complicated. The
doctors had been right. My nerves had
trouble communicating with muscles, I still
struggled with depression, and I had to
constantly adjust my medications. It truly
was a full-time job. I spent any spare time
returning favors to many deserving people
by giving free legal advice whenever it was
needed, and by lending a hand with fund-
raising and promotion for the greyhound
rescue group in Sedona. The days I was
forced to spend in bed became an accepted
part of my life — no longer did I rage
against it.

Over the next two years, Freddie and I
had our share of challenges. Sandoz, the
girlish golden who revered Freddie's every
step, had to be put down. Severe hip dysplasia had made it impossible for her to

even go outside to relieve herself. Freddie went into an emotional, teary funk. Comet was so distraught that she would walk to the neighbor's house where Sandoz had stayed during our travels, waiting at the front door for her sister to come out. Kylie and Lindsey were still angry with Freddie, pretty much precluding family gatherings. Jackie was more certain that happy days had finally arrived because she visited us regularly from Flagstaff, but it wasn't until Lindsey's June wedding in 2008 that the four women passed the peace pipe.

During this time, I developed a deep interest in cliff dwellings and other artifacts from the prehistoric cultures of Northern Arizona. It started when friends convinced me to take Comet for walks in the nearby canyons. I had never thought I'd be able to walk among the red rocks of Sedona, not even for short distances, but now I could. Comet trotted out in front, constantly sniffing the rocks and scrubby bushes. Seeing her stand motionless while staring at a far-off pack of coyotes reassured me that she wasn't planning on leaving me anytime soon.

Freddie left the time-share operation and found a new job as a real estate sales representative for a vacation resort. She now had a functioning spouse for social activities with friends, and we both loved going to the local clubs to hear live music. We acted like we had just met through some kind of dating service, constantly relearning things about each other that we never should have forgotten.

One warm spring day Comet and I were hiking with some friends when my cell phone vibrated. I figured it was a worried Freddie, making sure my buddies were taking good care of me. Instead, it was my daughter Lindsey calling from Omaha to tell me she was pregnant — our first grandchild would arrive in September. Freddie was more than willing to look for work in the health care profession back in Nebraska if that meant our grandchild would get to know us. She had trained so many cardiology nurses, medical students, and interns that she would have no trouble finding a flextime position in a cardiac unit. Freddie no longer wanted to work full-time managing her own unit. We were having too much fun. Social Security Disability benefits added to proceeds from a private disability policy would be enough to fill in the income gap.

It was a sign of our growing good luck that we had sold our home three months before the nationwide housing meltdown. In Sedona, prices had been especially inflated, and we made an extremely nice profit on the sale. After the bubble burst, we bought a small condo on a nearby golf course, which enabled us to live in two places again if we wanted to. And we weren't leaving Sedona permanently, only for the summers. That is, if Freddie could drag me away from Nebraska after we learned the baby would be a grand*daughter.* Freddie had her doubts about that.

Four years after Comet opened that hotel door in Albuquerque, making sure I had another chance at life, I sat gazing out of floor-to-ceiling windows overlooking the frozen lake that lay below our new Nebraska home. For the first time in years, the entire family was together for the Christmas holidays. My three girls exploded in laughter after a particularly raunchy joke from my mom. Lindsey's husband and Kylie's fiancé made sure the wine was flowing, eager to impress me with their fondness for my daughters. Freddie grinned at me from across the kitchen island and raised her glass in a brief, private toast.

Next to me on the living room floor, a months-long drama was reaching its conclusion. Since our return to Nebraska in May, Lindsey's little girl, Natalie, had been both curious about and fearful of Comet, who must have looked as big as a mastodon to her. Not in the least bit offended, Comet had bided her time, following Natalie at a safe distance all over the house. Now fifteen months old, Nat was almost as tall as Comet's legs, a stature that seemed to give the toddler confidence. For the past week I had watched as Natalie repeatedly approached Comet's bed, always turning back just before her hand touched the dog's head. Comet never moved or lifted her head, waiting as always with closed eyes and perked ears.

Finally Natalie plunked down onto the dog bed. Comet lifted her head in slow motion until her eyes were level with the little girl's face. As the seconds passed, Natalie visibly relaxed. She stretched her index finger forward, touching Comet's nose. The giggle that followed was clearly Natalie's way of saying, "Comet wants me to be her buddy!"

Because my recovery had been so rocky, Comet didn't surrender her service dog duties for some time. She still occasionally gave me a boost out of a chair or bed, especially when I was tired. After she made friends with Natalie, however, she was much more willing to consider retiring. Comet was now a public ambassador for the greyhound breed. Whenever we went out, people would gather to admire her. When I gave permission, she would slowly approach the nearest stranger, head high and doe eyes staring, to give them her special hug. For some reason, Comet comforted people and put them at ease. Within moments, strangers would start telling me about a childhood pet they often dreamed about, a son who was stationed in Afghanistan, or a wife who had passed away and was still missed. Otherwise unruly kids at the grocery store would quietly approach and politely ask to pet the exotic animal, invariably asking their mother, "Can we get one?"

Comet had apparently become a local celebrity, because in April of 2010 the Nebraska Humane Society honored her as "Service Dog of the Year." The Humane Society representative told me, "I met you and Comet when we were both at the doctor's office. When I brought her name up to the committee members, half of them already knew her."

I've never been able to find words that could adequately describe Comet's contented acceptance of the roller-coaster life she lived with me. I always had the feeling that she was trying to tell me something important, some piece of ancient wisdom that would make my struggles easier. The thought that Comet had lived several past lives was never far from the surface. I had been reading a modern translation of Cicero's *De senectute* when I found a passage that comes close to what I feel Comet's lesson might be:

The best Armour of Old Age is a well spent Life preceding it; a Life employed in the Pursuit of useful Knowledge, in honourable Actions and the Practice of Virtue; . . . because a Conscience bearing Witness that our Life was well spent, together with the Remembrance of past good Actions, yields an unspeakable Comfort to the Soul.

Now fourteen years old, Comet is feeling her age. Arthritis is visibly slowing her down. Her kidney functions are shaky. But it's pretty clear to me that my greyhound has an unspeakable comfort of the soul from her well-spent life. She pulls the bed-covers off me in the morning not to help me but to announce that it's time for her walk — the walks are for her now, not for me. She actually demands some attention from me, rubbing her head against me until I pet her and tell her she's pretty. Our routines are centered more around her schedule than mine, whether it's eating or exploring the neighborhood. Comet has spent enough time waiting for me. I now take her to the doctor rather than the reverse. She's earned every bit of my attention and more treats than I can provide in a lifetime. Comet is going to have the pampered retirement she so richly deserves.

Just when I think I have learned all I can from this remarkable animal, Comet lets me know there is no limit to love. My hips were shot after all the years of bearing the weight and stress that should have been absorbed by my spine, so I visited a new series of doctors to discuss a hip replacement. Comet deduced that something was up. Nervous, she began her former habit of stalking me through every room in the house, always at the ready. After successful hip-replacement surgery, Freddie and I returned home with crutches and a walker. That was all Comet needed to see. She trotted downstairs to the basement, and the sound of falling boxes told us she was in the storage area. Soon she came back up, carrying her old worn-out service harness. I didn't need it. She dropped it at my feet.

I'll never understand why this wonderful dog chose me. I'll never be able to fully comprehend the depth of forgiveness Comet displayed after the suffering she endured at the racetrack. I'll never know why a dog tried so hard for so long to remind me of the eternal values of love, loyalty, and the infinite expectation of dawn. But I'm long past wrestling with those enigmas. Instead, as Comet ages, I find myself replaying that day so long ago when she left sorrow and melancholy behind, suddenly intent on adopting a lonely and discouraged man. I remember how surprised I was and that I said out loud, "I think Comet likes me."

ACKNOWLEDGMENTS

There's an old Plains saying about risk taking: *Just make sure you know what fleas come with the dog.* Wise advice.

Thankfully, Betsy Amster fell in love with a flealess greyhound, ignoring the problems loitering at the other end of the leash. Whew! Lynette Padwa trusted her skills, confident she could stamp out dangerous infestations. You did. Amy Gash, your upbeat editorial disposition was the treatment that fleabag needed. At least I quit itching after you first, and then Jude Grant, worked your magic.

Some ignored wisdom, leaping without knowing. Louis Bayard, without your encouragement and the unwillingness to trash my initial draft, all of this would still be in my head. Sandi Ault, I'll find a way to repay your introduction of me to your agent, but thank you. Craig Johnson, your support was inspiring. As was Judy's. Anne Hillerman, thank you for befriending me during the incubation of this project. Thank you, Algonquin Books, for your tremendously supportive staff.

Some really had no choice. Mom, you're the toughest person I know. With your support and love, how could I not have made it to this point? Kylie, Lindsey, and Jackie — nothing has the potential to have more fleas than a father you didn't choose. I hope this book soothes some hurt, but my love for you — beautiful daughters all — has never wavered.

Some accepted the fleas. Like Comet, who risked infection simply because of her mind-blowing desire to save me. This book celebrates you.

Finally, a woman who looked at me and concluded, "What's the big deal with a few fleas anyway?" My life has been delightfully electrified ever since. *Je t'aime, Frederique.*

ABOUT THE AUTHOR

Steven D. Wolf is an active participant in greyhound advocacy. He divides his time between Omaha, Nebraska, and Sedona, Arizona.

The employees of Thorndike Press hope you have enjoyed this Large Print book. All our Thorndike, Wheeler, and Kennebec Large Print titles are designed for easy reading, and all our books are made to last. Other Thorndike Press Large Print books are available at your library, through selected bookstores, or directly from us.

For information about titles, please call:
  (800) 223-1244

or visit our Web site at:
  http://gale.cengage.com/thorndike

To share your comments, please write:
  Publisher
  Thorndike Press
  10 Water St., Suite 310
  Waterville, ME 04901